LIBERATING EDUCATION

psychological learning
through improvisational drama

Farnum Gray
&
George C. Mager

McCutchan Publishing Corporation
2526 Grove Street
Berkeley, California 94704

ABIGAIL E. WEEKS MEMORIAL LIBRARY
UNION COLLEGE
BARBOURVILLE, KENTUCKY

792.028
G778

Copyright 1973 by McCutchan Publishing Company
All rights reserved
Library of Congress Catalogue Card Number 73-7240
ISBN 0-8211-0609-0
Printed in the United States of America

For Wanda

CONTENTS

One:
IMPROVISATIONAL DRAMA:
THE FRAMEWORK

INTRODUCTION

In a year-end conversation, Wilt, a black, muscular twelve year-old, told us his improvisational drama course had been "meaningful." Asked what he meant, he gave what seemed like accurate perceptions of the changes in some of his classmates.

"But what about you?"

"Oh, yeah—me," he said. "Well, I've learned an awful lot."

"Can you tell me what you've learned?"

"No, no," Wilt groaned. "Man, it's all inside."

Although Wilt was telling us of the richness, depth, and unexpectedness of his experience in the course, he also reminded us of one of the difficulties of education by direct experience: you can't measure it. You also can't say in advance what students are supposed to learn, since that varies widely and unpredictably from one person to another.

If we had tried, at the beginning of the semester, to set goals for what Wilt would learn in the course, our goals would have been short of the development this ghetto boy actually experienced.

"The object of education is not to know but to live," Richard Boleslavsky wrote in *Acting: The First Six Lessons*.[1] In writing for acting students, Boleslavsky made a point that applies to all education. There is more to life than we can codify, and there is more to what people can get out of improvisational drama than what they "know." Like Wilt, every person has capacities and personality variations that are difficult to imagine, much less to plan for.

Experience with dramatic improvisation and movement has convinced us that these techniques enable people to develop the marvelously broad spectrum of their human capacities. A considerable

1

body of literature supports our experience that drama has enormous potential for freeing people to develop capacities they might not have known they had and teaching them to relate honestly and intimately to other people.

Many teachers see the need for this kind of learning. Yet most students have little, if any, opportunity in school to develop themselves through dramatic improvisation. We have talked with some teachers who for years had thought that dramatic improvisation was possibly the most important activity their classes could experience, but who had done very little with drama. These teachers did not know how to encourage and structure dramatic expression, and they assumed that to teach with drama would require theatrical talent and training they did not have. After participating in our improvisational drama workshops, they enthusiastically began teaching with drama. Dramatic improvisation is so important to individual development that it must not be left only to those teachers with acting talent and training. Every child should be provided with opportunities and techniques for becoming what he can be.

It became our overriding purpose to find ways to make effective teaching with drama practical for teachers. Educators who observed classes or took part in workshops urged us to put our experience into a book. In doing so, our essential purpose is to communicate enough of our experience with improvisational drama to enable teachers to make important additions to their repertoires of teaching approaches and techniques. At the same time, we hope to help school administrators and other policymakers understand what these approaches to learning offer and how they can be implemented.

We especially hope to convey something of what it is possible for kids to do. The expectations of many adults for problem-ridden inner-city kids—the subjects of most of our case material—are distressingly low. We hope readers will see that these kids, when given a safe, stimulating environment in which free expression is encouraged, are capable of strikingly creative, mature, and humane behavior.

The kids' performances stunned and exhilarated a respected clinical psychologist who observed a class at the time we were starting to plan this book. After the class, he groped for words to comment on what he had seen:

That's a liberal education. A liberating education. An emotionally liberating experience. Getting the meaning of it to other teachers will be difficult. How does one maximize the educational process for every child? This has something to do with it. It is fundamentally creative. I wish every teacher could have seen that class, just to see how creative children can be.

Such comments helped convince us that we should not only examine the principles of teaching with drama and give details on teaching techniques, but also try to communicate the actual experience. We wish to show what happens in a class, how it looks and sounds and feels, how the teacher's work affects students, and the growth that real people experience through improvisational drama. We hope that our concrete narrations will help readers gain understanding, perhaps even have insights that we did not have, through the close observation of fact.

Once the principles are understood and the reader has tasted the experience, the main value of specific exercises is to suggest ideas. We offer no sequence of lesson plans. You can't take students where they are if you're following a predetermined set of lessons. Instead, we show how the teacher can make plans based on the cues given by students.

The action from classes taught by George Mager is reproduced from audio tape recordings and notes taken by Farnum Gray, who observed from the back of the room. (We handle the awkward problem of dual authorship by referring to each other by our first names. The students' names have been changed to protect their privacy.)

Much of the case studies material here is from two groups of students at the Pennsylvania Advancement School in Philadelphia, where we worked for several years. The Advancement School was an independent developmental arm of the School District of Philadelphia. The students in the laboratory school were boys in the sixth, seventh, and eighth grades who had normal or better intelligence but had been achieving far below their capacities in public or parochial schools. Most came from low-income families, and at least 60 percent were black.

We have also used basically the same structure and approach in teaching improvisational drama to a wide range of other people, including primary and high school students, university undergraduates, graduate students, education instructors, public school teachers, counselors, and administrators. Improvisational drama facilitates the kinds of personal growth necessary for effective, humanistic teaching. Some of our most exciting experiences have been in the training of teachers.

Improvisational drama provides a versatile complex of tools for exploring many kinds of subject matter. These tools can be mixed with other approaches, including the time-tested academic methods, to enrich learning and vary activities. Even a few minutes of physical and expressive activities can pep up classes remarkably. Spot use of drama and movement will be most effective, though, if students have first developed these tools through a course lasting a few weeks, or months, or longer.

DEVELOPMENTAL EMPHASES OF IMPROVISATIONAL DRAMA

Our purpose in teaching is to afford people opportunities to develop their human capacities fully. Our approach and premises are based on theories of developmental psychology.

In 1895, John Dewey wrote the definitive statement of the purpose of education based on developmental psychology: "Education is precisely the work of *supplying the conditions* which will enable the psychical functions, as they successively arise, to mature and pass into higher functions in the freest and fullest manner."

As Dewey states, the natural development of a person's "psychical functions"—or personal capacities—has different focuses that "successively arise" at different ages. For example, consider some of the focuses of development that arise in young children from five through seven.

Young children gain some of their most important development through symbolic play. Jean Piaget writes,

Practically every form of psychological activity is initially enacted in play. At any rate, play constitutes a functional exercise of these activities. Cognitive activity thus initiates play, and play in turn reinforces cognitive activity. . . . [a] form of play very characteristic of young children . . . employs thought, but thought that is almost entirely idiosyncratic and has a minimum of collective elements. This is symbolic play or imaginative and imitative play, [in which the child] remakes his own life as he would like it to be. He relives all his pleasures, resolves all his conflicts. Above all, he compensates for and completes reality by means of a fiction.[2]

Sara Smilansky, professor of psychology at the University of Tel Aviv in Israel, writes that many "socially disadvantaged" children have little of this kind of play and need much more if they are to be able to cope with contemporary problems. Research of the Harvard School of Education's Pre-School Project tends to corroborate

Smilansky's conclusion. Throughout that study, "middle-class youngsters were found role-playing five times more frequently than lower-class children of the same age."[3]

"It is my opinion," Smilansky writes, "that children denied the opportunity to learn sociodramatic play will have less chance to learn how to accept a problematic world." She suggests that, to be able to cope with the world in adulthood, the child in a rapidly changing society needs more of this kind of play than does the child in a stable, traditional society. According to her studies, "Sociodramatic play behavior develops three main aspects in a child":

1. *Creativity*, based on utilization of past experience and controlled by the demands of some framework.

2. *Intellectual growth*, which includes power of abstraction, widening of concept and acquisition of new knowledge.

3. *Social skills*, which includes positive give and take, tolerance and consideration.[4]

Now let us consider a focus of development important in adolescence, that turbulent time when the person attempts to discover himself, to define himself in relation to his environment—to formulate an identity that will not be repudiated by the world around him. David Beres suggests the desirability of the child entering adolescence in a "state of uncertainty, facing difficulty and serious conflicts, and emerging from it with stable, socially acceptable patterns of responses that we recognize as character."[5] In fact, should the child formulate an identity too quickly—that is, become set too early in his development—he may not have tested various solutions to conflicts or investigated the alternative paths open to him, and he might become frozen at a low level in the development of his capacities.

Inhelder and Piaget suggest that adolescence is that age when the adolescent takes his place in adult society and formulates his personality by adopting adult roles.[6] Erik Erikson points out that in seeking to establish an identity the adolescent often takes on roles, or "temporarily overidentifies with the hero of cliques and crowds to the point of an apparently complete loss of individuality."[7] By projecting his "diffused self-image" onto another, the adolescent can actually see it reflected, and he hopes eventually to clarify his image by this process. Young people also often take on what society would term negative roles out of a fear of losing their identity. This "taking on" of roles, according to Erikson, allows the adolescent to come to grips with the ideas and ideals that will be the basis for his way of life.

According to Erikson, the formation of intimate relationships during the adolescent years is essential if one is to avoid becoming an isolated person.

[When] a youth does not accomplish such intimate relationships with others—and, I would add, with his own inner resources—in late adolescence or early adulthood, he may settle for highly stereotyped interpersonal relations,

resulting in isolation. Erikson also states that forming intimate relationships is necessary if the adolescent is to avoid "distantiation: the readiness to repudiate, isolate, and, if necessary, destroy those forces and people whose essence seems dangerous to one's own."[8]

In the preceding pages we have looked at parts of the developmental focuses at two different ages. For other age groups, the focus is on development of other personal capacities. Regardless of the ages and developmental needs of students, growth can be expected to occur if they exercise their capacities in four areas of development, which we term *physical freeing, concentration, believability,* and *relationships.* These are the emphases in our teaching of improvisational drama. In structuring classes, we provide opportunities for development in these four areas.

We believe that experience in these four areas will help a person to develop whatever functions are arising at that particular time in his life. This development occurs in the young child's idiosyncratic re-creation of reality, with its attendant creative, intellectual, and social growth; in the adolescent's trying out of different identities; or in the adult's freeing himself from physical inhibition and gaining spontaneity.

Growth through improvisational drama is a natural development of capacities that are already there, *needing* to be exercised and developed. The intervention of the teacher and the processes he uses should not impose beliefs, knowledge, or personal characteristics valued by the teacher or school administrator. Nor should they try to "speed up" the student's development, as in helping the adolescent to finish forming his identity at a younger age so he can choose his career and get a head start in preparing for it. Intervention should be intended only to *optimize* development for which the student has innate capacities and needs.

In using improvisational drama, the teacher does not try to *make* people be physically free, concentrate, be believable, or have better or more open or sensitive relationships. He does not teach students step by step how to do it; instead he provides a structure that enables them to develop in the four areas. The content explored within this structure is provided by the student. Often, the content is the self.

Our ways of teaching with improvisational drama enable people to explore alternative ways of being. We do not presuppose that there is one healthy, good way for people to be, but we do assume that the healthy person is flexible, free to choose among alternatives. Carl Jung's educational concerns are similar to ours when he writes,

We need not concern ourselves so much with the amount of specific information a child takes away with him from school; the thing of vital importance is that the school should succeed in freeing the young man from unconscious identity with his family, and should make him properly conscious of himself. Without this consciousness, he will never know what he really wants, but will always remain dependent and imitative, with the feeling of being misunderstood and suppressed.[9]

We use improvisational drama to help students learn procedures with which they can begin to free themselves and better understand themselves and others. We hope that they will become actively involved in processes of perceptual growth that will continue throughout their lives.

Such learning is usually called affective, but it includes skills of perception, understanding, communication, and personal effectiveness. In this case, we think the distinction between affective and cognitive has little, if any, value. When a student is using his body, voice, choice of words, past experience, and imagination to communicate with other people, who can distinguish between the affective and cognitive components of the process?

NO PSYCHIATRY

The improvisational drama teacher concentrates on the four basic areas of personal development: physical freeing, concentration, believability, and relationships. He does not teach psychological values, and he does not analyze students' experiences and tell them what they should learn about themselves from the experiences.

This point must be underscored because of the frequent confusion of improvisational drama with psychodrama, as practiced by J. L. Moreno and others, and the psychotherapeutic use of role playing. Although professionals who use psychodrama might learn something about structuring, pacing, and mixture of movement and drama from our work, they also have their own tools that should not be used by teachers who do not have psychiatric training. For example, a therapist might say to a patient, "You are troubled about your father. We will work on this problem by acting it out." Someone else might then play the role of the father, as the patient has described him, while the patient plays himself. The performance is analyzed immediately afterwards with the collaboration of the patient. This should *not* be done by teachers who are not trained therapists. The tools we work with and describe in this book are safe and effective for teachers to use in schools.

Needless to say, there are still those who maintain that expression of feelings and dealing with controversial matters have no place in the schools. That is absurd. There is no way for teachers to avoid affecting the deep-seated feelings of their students. The way for the teacher to play it safe is not to keep the lid tight, but to know what he is doing.

SOME BENEFITS

We follow students carefully as they move from class to class, observing the sharpening of perceptions and positive changes they experience. Seeing them come face-to-face with their own concepts of themselves is often a moving experience. Many discover that they are more capable than they thought. Some find that they can have warm, rewarding relationships with other people by behaving differently from their usual manner. We have held our breaths as black and white confronted each other with their real feelings about race. We have seen tight, glassy-eyed boys come alive in vital expressions of their fantasy lives, and frenetically hostile boys learn to make positive use of their energies.

From experienced educators who have gone through our inservice programs come comments such as:

"One of the most fascinating and memorable summers of my entire life."

"I feel there is now a way to reach kids. To give them opportunities to find out what's wrong and try to correct it. Traditional teaching methods could not allow this in the typical classroom situation."

"The program helped me to experience more fully what the function of a class can be: to allow a pupil to achieve more self-awareness, be freer to see himself in relation to the rest of the world, and to realize his own primal energies which are the delight of being and thinking."

"As a teacher, I feel that I can narrow the generation gap through improvisational drama."

"The improvisational drama workshop injected new light into my thinking about education. It has influenced all of my work since then, and I feel sure that improvisational drama will continue to be increasingly important."

A few educators whose acquaintance with improvisational drama is slight have vaguely felt that any approach that is not explicitly academic must somehow conflict with the learning of the three R's. Our experience convinces us that the opposite is true: the holistic development that takes place through improvisational drama aids academic achievement.

When students achieve a state of growth in which they feel free, with inappropriate defenses inoperative, and are better able to concentrate, they can better absorb themselves in learning and creating. In our experience, learning that takes place in this state of creative absorption is of a very high level. The knowledge gained is likely to stick with the learner and be accessible at appropriate times in the form of useful, perhaps creative, associations.

In our work with urban junior high school underachievers, we found that improvisational drama stimulates improvement in verbal facility. We think that this improvement stems as much from the increased confidence of students and the shedding of inhibitions as from the stimulating verbal activity.

After a group of educators mostly black and with many years of experience in the Philadelphia school system—had observed one of George's classes, they made such comments as, "I never thought I would hear culturally deprived junior high school kids speaking so clearly and animatedly. Their vocabularies are amazing." This verbal improvement seems to extend not only to talking, but also to reading. The small amount of available data indicates that students' reading progress was substantially better than normal while they were taking improvisational drama.

TEACHING STYLES

No teacher should try to be exactly like any other. But teachers who cultivate their teaching artistry are always interested in studying good teaching—just as Picasso studied the techniques and style of Cezanne, not to imitate them, but to enrich his own highly personal artistry. This book gives some insights about teaching style that are relevant to any educator, including ways of projecting vitality in the classroom, remaining open to the group while providing the strength to make students feel safe, and keeping purposeful order without repressing students.

In particular, we believe that our ways of teaching resolve the needless conflict of extremes between those who think teachers must control and direct almost everything students do and those who think the teacher should become what Jonathan Kozol censoriously calls "a human inductive fan" by abdicating responsibility for what students do. We find that students can feel free and have permissiveness of expression while sustaining a sense of purpose and order. In our classes the teacher does have authority, but he limits his use of authority, competently and rationally, using it to structure the class so that the students can cooperate on challenging and sensitive tasks. There is no need to choose between repression and chaos.

WHO CAN TEACH THIS WAY?

As we have already noted, talent in acting and movement are not necessary for teaching improvisational drama, although they can be helpful. In addition, the teacher does not need to be a psychiatrist; indeed, it is essential that he not imagine himself one. What, then, are the qualities a teacher needs to teach with drama?

Basically, they are the same qualities one needs to be a good teacher: caring deeply about one's work, being keenly aware of the students and caring about them, being nonjudgmental and, of course, having energy and the ability to think on one's feet. Obviously, there are people who should not teach with drama, and there are people who should not be teaching at all. For the most part, they are the same people.

Teachers first starting to work with drama soon overcome the main stumbling block of self-consciousness. The awareness of not using drama with a great deal of nicety might bother them at first, but they find that as long as they heed the fundamentals their classes go well anyway. With experience comes confidence and refinement, and meeting the new challenges brings new rewards.

FOOTNOTES

1. Richard Boleslavsky, *Acting: The First Six Lessons* (New York: Theater Art Books, 1963), p. 48.

2. Jean Piaget, "The Mental Development of the Child," in *Six Psychological Studies* (New York: Vintage Books, 1968), p. 23.

3. Maya Pines, "Why Some 3-Year-Olds Get A's—And Some Get C's," *New York Times Magazine,* 6 July 1969, p. 12.

4. Sara Smilansky, "Can Adults Facilitate Play in Children?: Theoretical and Practical Considerations," in *The Child Strives Toward Self-Realization* (Washington, D.C.: National Association for the Education of Young Children, 1971), pp. 42-43.

5. David Beres, "Character Formation," in *Adolescents: Psychoanalytic Approach to Problems and Therapy,* ed. Sandor Lorand and Henry I. Schneer (New York: Dell, 1961), p. 2.

6. Barbel Inhelder and Jean Piaget, *The Growth of Logical Thinking From Childhood to Adolescence* (New York: Basic Books, 1958).

7. Erik Erikson, *Identity: Youth and Crisis* (New York: W. W. Norton & Co., 1968), p. 132.

8. Ibid., p. 136.

9. Carl G. Jung, *Psychology and Education* (Princeton, N.J.: Princeton University Press, 1954), pp. 46-47.

Two:
A MIRROR FOR
JELLYROLL JONES

Teaching interns who have taken our course have called improvisational drama "pure teaching," and in a sense it is. The teacher does not have the scholarly job of providing content. He concentrates on "teaching"—or structuring—the class. The teacher provides structure by handling students in such a way that their own content is likely to emerge and they can explore it. As the course progresses and the students learn about structure, they lead some of their own classes.

In improvisational drama, the content is relevant to the students because they generate it. Instead of prescribing the content, the teacher allows it to occur.

A person's feelings and the perceptions that determine his feelings and actions often are the most important subject for his education. This was true of Jellyroll Jones, a stocky, brown-skinned 12-year-old. For him, the most relevant content was his own hostility, and that was the content he brought forth and explored within the structure of his improvisational drama course.

The emotions and perceptions are so neglected by most schools that many people can't imagine how a student could benefit from emotional and perceptual education. Jellyroll's case should help clear up the mystery, and it should also give a concrete idea of what improvisational drama is.

Jelly had good teachers and a consistently stimulating program at the Pennsylvania Advancement School, and his experiences outside the improvisational drama class contributed to the progress he made.

When Jellyroll arrived at the Advancement School to begin his fourteen-week session, he was an extrovert—a very physical young man who did not know how to express himself physically. To get attention, he hit, bumped, and grabbed people. He seldom talked in a conversational tone, but shouted frantically as if he had to be heard quickly before everyone disappeared. Waiting his turn never occurred to him, as though he knew his turn would never come. This behavior is common among inner-city boys, and Jelly seemed largely unaware of the annoyance he caused other people. His teachers soon realized that feelings about race had something to do with Jellyroll's bumptiousness, but he had learned to avoid talking about racial matters.

For his teachers to force Jellyroll to suppress his feelings and study the conventional subject matter would have been absurd. He would not learn much if his energies were concentrated on trying to appear passive while he seethed with aggressive feelings.

Jelly took to improvisational drama from the start. In the early classes, much of the activity involved movement to music. Jelly could really move and groove, and he knew it. The dancing helped him build confidence that carried over into the dramatic improvisations, and his acting often sparkled.

Because it suspends the superiority of students who excel in literacy skills, improvisational drama is very well suited to culturally and racially mixed classes. Children from poor backgrounds are not at their usual disadvantage; in fact, their lives in the crowded slums often provide colorful and powerful dramatic material.

Jelly became so fascinated with improvisational drama (ID) that he was the first in his class to volunteer to teach. On a Friday, George assigned him to lead the warm-ups on the following Tuesday. On Tuesday morning, we sleepily dragged into the Advancement School at 7:20 to conduct an ID workshop for counselors from other schools. There was Jellyroll, an hour and forty minutes before school was to start, lying on the floor writing in a notebook. He was outlining his plan for the warm-ups. He was excited but seemed neither scared nor cocky. He was making his plans with a workmanlike attitude that seemed different from his earlier behavior at the school.

The plans were good. Jelly led the warm-ups with poise and vitality, and his classmates threw themselves into it. In discussion, the boys said Jelly's warm-ups were better than George's had ever been. George had to admit that enthusiasm had been higher than in any of the group's previous warm-ups. Jelly felt good about the boys in the class. They could have balked and made him look bad, but instead they had helped him.

Sometimes Jelly thought ID was great, but other times he was not so sure. As several other students have done, he twice went to George and said he might not come to class the next day. "That is your decision to make," George told him. "I can't make it for you." Jelly always showed up for class. In saying that he might skip class, Jelly was actually asking George to protect him from discomfort. George did not give him that guarantee, but the fascination of learning about himself consistently overcame the fear of what he might learn and kept Jelly in the class.

In the fourth week of the session Jellyroll and his classmates sat watching improvisations on cushions along two sides of a square patch of floor that served as a stage. The room was dark except for a spotlight on center stage. The class had started with warm-ups, in which vigorous physical activity alternated with deep relaxation. Then there was an improvisation in which Doug tried to convince his pal not to become a teacher. The pal was played by one of Doug's teachers, and Doug expressed a general hatred for pedagogy.

Then George introduced the second improvisation: "This is Sister Fran. Okay, Ray, you've got to convince Sister Fran not to be a nun."

"She's a nun already."

"Right. You've got to convince her not to be one. All right, get your tension up. Concentrate. Think about it. Become specific."

Sister Fran Tobin had brought a group of sisters from her school, Sacred Heart Academy of Albany, New York, for a brief visit to learn about ID and other Advancement School techniques. She had been in George's improvisational drama class for teachers at the Advancement School the previous summer, and George had asked her to take part in this class as a student. Her colleagues observed from the dark at the back of the room, along with fourteen public school educators.

As the improvisation started, Ray fidgeted in his checked sport coat and could not look Sister Fran in the eye. He had talked several times of how nuns had beaten him, preached at him, and otherwise abused him when he had attended Catholic schools, and he could hardly believe that George had put him on the stage with a hated nun.

"Hi, Ray."

"Hi. I hear you want to be a nun."

"Yeah. I do."

"Well, that's stupid."

Ray started out stiffly. He was usually rather stiff and unexpressive. As he continued heaping insults on the nun, however, he warmed up and became believable.

"Listen," Sister Fran said, "suppose I'm your sister, and you know I really want to be a nun. Are you going to tell me it's stupid?"

"I'd say, *forget* it!"

"Why would you tell me to forget it, if you know I really want to be a nun and nothing else?"

In an anguished voice, Ray cried, "Because you waste your life that way!"

From simply hating nuns, he had moved to criticizing the institution of nunnery. There was real communication and budding friendship for the rest of their improvisation. But it was the hostility Ray had showered on the nun earlier that lighted up Jelly's square face and made him bounce on his cushion. George saw Jelly's excitement, and during the next improvisation, he changed his lesson plan and devised a situation that would get Jelly on that stage to let it all out.

In the next improvisation one "actor" was assigned to convince another that he should quit school to run numbers and push drugs. Jelly and his classmates liked it. They groaned when George yelled, "Freeze," to end it. Smiling, George extended his hand to Jellyroll, who hopped up and stepped into the spotlight. George said, "Jelly is a black power leader—black militant. Okay?"

Then George gave a hand to Frank, a bright, sensitive white boy who was disheartened by the hostility Jellyroll and some of his black friends were showing for whites. "You've got to convince Jelly not to be a black militant," George instructed Frank. "Get your tension up," he told the boys. "Get your concentration. Okay? Here we go."

"I've heard a lot of rumors about you," Frank said.

Bouncing jauntily, Jelly snapped, "Like what?"

"You're going to get yourself in trouble. Going to make yourself a big man."

"That's right!" Jelly grinned and smacked his chewing gum. The tension was real and electric.

"Well, what's the difference between black and white? Can you tell me that?"

"Soul brothers," Jelly said haughtily.

"Soul?"

Jelly leaned forward and crooned, "So-o-o-o-oul."

"Well, I don't care what religion or anything anybody is," Frank said, pretending not to understand what kind of soul Jelly meant. "They're still just the same inside, and I think . . . ."

"That's what you think!" Jelly cut in.

"Look, did you ever see . . . uh . . . look in the news and see pictures of how the cops are beating the crap out of you guys 'cause you keep on bothering, running around, demonstrating, making trouble. Have you ever seen them? They go downtown. Break up and rob everything. You don't want to be like that, do you?"

Coolly, Jellyroll said, "Your soul do not like us."

Frank looked agitated: "Yeah. As I remember kidding you . . . going to church, you were pretty nice; but all of a sudden you've changed. You . . ."

"I still go to church."

"Yeah, but still you . . ."

". . . once in a while." Jelly grinned arrogantly.

"Yeah! Once in a while! You're a hypocrite!"

"Ha, ha!" Jelly's laugh was half growl.

Frank said, "And look at the clothes you're wearing!"

"They're all right. Look at yours. Red socks!" Jelly shouted gleefully. He grabbed the neckband of Frank's long red underwear and jerked frenetically, crying, "Yeah, yeah, yeah!"

"Freeze."

George had to enforce a structure that would keep the class physically safe. But he had to do it without making Jelly feel slapped down. To say, "You mustn't grab people, Jellyroll," might have caused a sullen withdrawal, extinguishing the spark that had been growing in Jelly since the start of warm-ups. But stopping the improvisation at that point would leave Frank feeling frustrated; he was too sensitive to be unaware of the implications of Jelly grabbing his long underwear, which to the black boy was a symbol of the white working class. Instead of passing judgment on what they had done, George simply reminded the boys of the existing structure. "All right, you're forgetting your tasks," he said evenly, as the boys held their positions. "What's your task? What do you have to accomplish up there? Get back to it. Move."

"I know I have long johns on," Frank said. "It's cold outside. But what's this black socks! What's that for?"

"The leader!" Jellyroll said proudly.

"And you're walking around every day like this." Frank imitated Jelly's strut. "And you're always starting trouble in school—and mostly with white kids."

"Ahr-r-r-r. So what?"

"What is it with you? What do you want to be one of them for? All you want to do is start trouble and everything. There's no particular kid's color or anything."

"There ain't?" Jelly said with a marvelous sneer.

"There ain't, as you put it. Big deal. Wow! White trash, right? You don't really mean this stuff," Frank said, grasping Jelly's shoulder and shaking him.

"Yes I do!"

"I'm not messing with you any more. If you're smart, you'll knock it off." They circled each other suspiciously and Frank said, "You know something, you're going to get yourself in a lot of trouble. Just keep it up!"

"Freeze."

George shook the boys' hands, and, with arms around their shoulders, guided them back to their seats. "Great acting," he said.

Jellyroll was not sure how much of what he had done was acting and how much was real. There was some of each in his performance, he felt, and he could think about it later. In the meantime, he basked in the appreciation of his classmates, who had been spellbound. Jelly had a good feeling about Frank, since the two of them had pulled off the success together.

Jelly was now being aggressive in a new way. He was using his aggressiveness; it was not using him. It was not frustration taking him over; he was being aggressive because he wanted to.

George had paired Jelly and Frank because he thought their interests could complement each other in the right kind of situation. Had he been wrong, the boys probably would have gotten something out of the exercise anyhow. As long as the teacher does not try to tell the students what makes them tick and how they ought to change, there is no harm done if the teacher is wrong, although a teacher who usually guesses right can plan improvisations that will more effectively help students develop. It is not necessary for a teacher to decide whether a student is acting or expressing his own feelings; this ambiguity gives many students a sense of security that enables them to express feelings they might not admit even to themselves.

The class continued. "New task," George told the group. "Think of something that you're afraid of. Now become specific in your head. You must come up here and show us fear. Now concentrate specifically on what you could be afraid of. Now wait a minute, that's only half the job. Sometimes, while one person's up here being afraid of something, I will go to somebody else and tap him on the shoulder. His job is to go up and help the person who is afraid—help him not to be afraid."

George guided Cathy into the spotlight. She was a tall, blonde Antioch College student who worked at the school, and she and Jelly were good friends. Cathy crouched on the floor, trembling, face in hands. Then George tapped Jelly's shoulder. He swaggered up to the huddled girl and cracked, "Are you doing your yoger exercises?"

Jellyroll wanted very much to cheer Cathy up. But in his brusque efforts, he jerked her to her feet and banged her against the wall. When she remained frightened, he pounded his fist against the wall and shouted gutturally, "What's the matter with you?"

After the exercise, Jelly and Cathy sat on the floor in the spotlight and the boys talked about what had happened. One said, "I think Jelly must have been feeling pretty frustrated, you know."

After they had talked awhile, George said, "Tell me this somebody: Did you think he was helping Cathy? Yes or no?"

"No!" the boys chorused.

"He seemed to be scaring her more," Robby said. "When he got angry, she got even more scared."

George said, "Jelly, do you think there is an alternative way of doing this? Can you? Try it. Now this time—you may play it as you like—but this time you must try a different approach. Let's see if that's more successful."

Cathy started as before, but this time Jelly was gentle and concerned. In the discussion afterwards, the class remarked on the difference. "He helped her this time," one boy said. "This sure was better," Cathy said. "When he got angry at me, the first time, it made me more scared. When he didn't seem to get upset because I was scared, it was much easier."

Then Sister Fran was the scared one, and Ray, who minutes before had tried to convince her not to be a nun, was supposed to help her. In the discussion that followed, Jellyroll had some very definite opinions on how to help.

Late that afternoon, Jelly happily ran up to George. While talking to him, he punched his shoulder and pulled on his arm. George said, "Jelly, do I like you?"

"Yeah."

"Are you sure that I like you?"

"Yeah."

"Then you don't have to hit me any more."

Jelly got that look kids get when they've just seen the light.

Talking about drama, Jelly said he'd learned a lot that day about a different way to act in class.

"Drama isn't limited to the classroom," George said. "You can be different outside the class, too."

That look spread over Jelly's face again. Maybe he didn't have to be rough, tough Jellyroll Jones any more.

On Monday George found a typed note on his desk:

YE OLDE STORY
TO GEORGE MAGOR, (ye olde DR teach)
on the 27th day and the 11th month
we JELLY and GEORGE had a little talk about class
and over the week end I thought a-
bout it and I really appreciate it.
YE OLDe STUDENT JELLY

In the days that followed, both adults and students praised Jelly for his striking improvement in consideration for other people. Eventually, he became everybody's buddy. In the chain reaction exercises, Jelly took many opportunities to drape an arm around someone's neck and call him friend. It was unreal. In trying to find who he was through trial and error, he went to the opposite extreme.

There was a second note, as obsequious as the first had been sincere.

Dear George

I really appreciated your kindness. Your class yesterday, I think that was the best class I ever went to. Georr ge will you please lead the class today?

I was really happy yesterday when I helped you and Dan.

thanks

One day, there was an improvisation in which Herb Katz, a teacher who was visiting the class, timidly asked his boss for a raise, saying that he had not had one in years and that he really needed the money. George's instructions were that anyone who wanted to help Herb could step into the improvisation. Jelly and several others went to Herb's rescue. The others wanted to help Herb become more assertive in talking with his boss, but Jelly—acting overbearingly friendly—wanted to steal some money and give it to Herb. In the discussion, some of the boys criticized Jelly's superficial approach. They thought he was not helping Herb, but only encouraging him to delay dealing with his real problem, his timidity. Herb thought so, too. Jelly was puzzled, and he thought seriously about the criticism he received.

One day while he was acting, Jelly looked to the teacher for praise. George said, "Do it for you, not for us." It was an intimate statement, showing that George cared enough to understand Jelly beyond his expectations. Jelly learned from it, although he probably would have resisted if it had seemed like standardized advice.

The "new Jellyroll Jones" was starting to pall. Now that the magic formula of superniceness had failed, what *did* he want to be? Jelly began analyzing things. He observed and listened to people keenly. He still had a strong need for affection, but he was going after it in more mature ways. By this time he was convinced that his teachers and classmates liked him and cared about him. He became more concerned about being proud of himself than about impressing others. Once, in discussing an improvisation done by some other boys, Jelly said, "These kids are trying to please you, George. Every time they get on the stage they start looking at you." His comment showed improvement both in understanding people's actions and in honestly saying what he thought.

Like a number of other kids who have taken improvisational drama, Jelly often articulated what he had learned from his own experiences while discussing the actions of the other boys. All aspects of the class were part of the structure within which Jellyroll Jones explored himself and his potential.

One morning, George walked into the classroom and announced, "I'm not here today." Then he walked to the back of the room and sat down. Two boys volunteered to lead the class. After a while, the other boys got bored with the rather dull leadership and acclaimed Jelly as their teacher for the rest of the hour.

Jelly set up an improvisation in which two black boys were

supposed to criticize each other's clothes. Chet was open in his expressions of powerful anti-white feelings, while Doug tended to butter up whites. Their argument over clothes became a bitter, personal clash over attitudes toward white people. Throughout the drama, Jelly squatted beside the stage and leaned forward, observing with rapt intensity. Was he using the situation to externalize his own internal conflict? We cannot really know, and we do not need to know.

Through his Advancement School experience, Jelly had become actively involved in a process of perceptual growth, which was changing him from a destructively aggressive person to one who could assert himself constructively. If he can continue this perceptual growth throughout his life, it will have been more important to him than anything he could have learned from a seventh-grade textbook.

Within the improvisational drama structure, students learn to practice an experiential way of thinking. The perpetual question for them is, What do I do with this experience?

An experience strikes a chord of meaning within a person. This is an internal process. The teacher structures the external situation in which the experience can occur and encourages freedom and helpfulness among the students, but he does not interpret the experience for the students or evaluate the content the student brings to the activity.

George never told Jellyroll he could not do something. As Jelly gained new perceptions, he made his own decision to stop abusing people. Had George simply told him to stop hitting people, shut up, and be still, Jelly probably would have felt threatened and clung to the perceptions he already had, and his behavior would have rigidified. Instead, when George gave Jelly his instructions for the second improvisation with Cathy, for example, the requirement that he "must try a different approach" was perceived by Jelly as a challenge rather than a threat. Rather than narrowing his vision, as he might have if he had felt threatened, he rose to meet the challenge by creating a new, more successful mode of behavior for himself.

"To be good is noble," Mark Twain wrote, "but to teach others to be good is nobler—and less trouble." It also borders on the impossible. If a student is told that he should care about other people, he might learn that concern is held in high regard, but he does not necessarily feel concern for other people. People usually do what they perceive to be right, and the most effective way for them to make constructive changes in the way they act is to sharpen their perceptions through experience. As students learn to value their own experience, rather than merely paying lip service to what they are told, hypocrisy diminishes.

In examining one part of the development of a twelve-year-old black "underachiever" from an inner-city slum, we have tended to look through only one "psychological stencil." There are quite a few of these psychological stencils, replete with verbal labels, and teachers can benefit from knowing some of them. (Knowing only one is often worse than knowing none.) But for growing children, the verbal labels seem unnecessary.

The student selects from the experience those elements that are of the most value to him. And he selects only what he is ready and able to learn. If the teacher decides what is to be learned, the student might push aside realizations that are more important and relevant to himself in order to focus on the teacher's concerns. Before a student's question can be answered, he must in some way have asked the question. If a student is ready to accept interpretation from a teacher, he will give a cue that he is very close to the answer himself and would like another person's interpretation.

The teacher is not trying to learn something about the student and then teach it to him. He is trying to structure the classroom experience in such a way that the student learns how to learn about himself, as well as about other people and about how people interact.

Format is one important part of the structure of the class. In our courses, our usual format goes like this:

1. Warm-ups
2. Short improvisations or simple exercises
3. Richer, or longer, improvisations
4. The closing

However, format is for each teacher to decide. The most important concept in structuring is this:

The teacher provides structure by handling students in such a way that their own content is likely to emerge, and they can explore it.

Three:
ACTING:
THE FUNDAMENTAL
INSTRUMENT

Love the art in yourself, not yourself in the art. —Stanislavski

Although the class consisted of impromptu actions by a group made up mostly of seventh-grade underachieving boys, it was an electrifying theatrical experience. Nineteen observers, including some eminent educators, were amazed at the dramatic expressiveness of the students.

"I only hope the kids got as much out of it as they gave to me," one man said. "It was damn good theater."

"It *was* good theater," George agreed. "And what that means is that everything was working. And when everything is working, they have to be getting something out of it."

In improvisational drama, we are more concerned with the student's ability to use his personal resources than with the stage techniques he develops. Yet when a student moves his audience with a believable acting performance, you can be sure that he has gained something important from the experience.

Why is believable acting such an effective activity for learning? First, consider the tools an actor uses. They are within himself: his body, his mind, his experience, his perceptions, his vocabulary, and any other knowledge or skill he might bring to the creation of his performance. To give a convincing performance, the actor must be familiar with these tools. The more aware a person is of his body, and the more he understands his own experience, the better he will be able to use them in his creation of a convincing portrayal.

Boleslavsky writes: "Concentration and observation, experience and memory, movement and poise, creation and projection—an actor must make them all the servants of his talent." Those are good servants for people other than actors to have, too.

ABIGAIL E. WEEKS MEMORIAL LIBRARY
UNION COLLEGE
BARBOURVILLE, KENTUCKY

That any of these talents could become the servants of Ray's development seemed unlikely at the start of the semester. His blue eyes were usually glazed over, and he seemed stiff, withdrawn, even somewhat autistic. But in a class that was good theater throughout, Ray's improvisation was outstanding.

After the warm-ups—in which the students' vitality indicated that they were ready for an "up" day—George said, "We've got to believe what we're doing. Can you take something and make us believe whatever you're doing with it?" He put an old felt hat on the floor in the spotlight. "Think about it. What can you do with it? How can you make us believe in what you're doing?"

After two boys had done amusing improvisations with the hat, leaving it too bedraggled for further use, George substituted a smoking pipe. Our Antioch colleague, Cathy, went first and, predictably, got stoned.

Then it was Robby's turn. To help him he chose Carole, a counselor at another school who was taking the course to learn the techniques. Robby drew a lot of laughs as an obtuse husband, home from a business trip, who finds another man's pipe in his bedroom.

Ray excitedly volunteered to go next. He immediately held out his hand to George and asked him to assist. This was not surprising, since Ray and George had developed a close relationship. A few days earlier, Ray had told George that he was the first teacher he had ever trusted. He even said that George was a good guy.

As George waited at the back corner of the stage, Ray picked up the pipe. "Hey, nice pipe! All messed up, though. Better shine it up." As Ray rubbed the pipe with his sleeve, George figured out what was expected of him. He swirled out of his corner and bowed to Ray with a flourish.

"Yes, Master."

Ray lit up and gasped, "Oh, boy!" He really was delighted.

"Your wish is my command, Master."

"Which wish?"

"Whatever you wish."

"Who are you?"

"I'm from the pipe."

"But who are you?"

"I'm your servant."

"Since when?"

"Since you rubbed the pipe."

Ray looked genuinely incredulous and said, "Any wish is your command?"

"Anything you would like."

"Anything?"

"Anything!"

"I gotta think now," Ray said. He thought for a moment and then giggled.

"What would you like?" George asked.

"That you'd get back in there," Ray said with a laugh.

Still deadpan, George said, "You want me to get back in there? Just say, 'I wish for you to go back into the pipe,' and I will go back."

"I wish for you to go back into the pipe."

George smoothly contracted his body into a knot on the floor. Ray looked into the pipe and said with concern, "Jinni? You still in there? I'd like you to come out now."

George rose again. "Yes, Master."

"Could you take me on an adventure?"

"Yes, sir. Where would you like to go?"

"A castle!"

George asked where he'd like it to be, and while Ray pondered, George suggested Ireland.

"That sounds great! Yeah-h-h!"

"Just hold my arm." George swung Ray smoothly around the stage, stopped, and said, "There it is. That's yours, Master."

Ray gawked with his whole body. "You mean you're giving that to me!" he exclaimed.

"This is yours. It's all yours."

"It's mine?"

"You may do as you wish with it."

"All mine!"

"All yours."

"Oh, man!" Ray was breathless as he ran into the castle. "C'mon."

Grandly, George said, "This is the living room."

Goggle-eyed, Ray said, "It's *very* nice!"

"It's very *big,* Master," the jinni said matter of factly. "Bedrooms? There are twelve bedrooms."

Ray whistled. He was seeing everything, and he was making the whole physical setting believable to the audience.

". . . and six bathrooms."

"How many balconies?"

"Every room has its own balcony," George said. "Come out back, and I'll show you the rear view."

They stepped to a rear balcony. With a grand wave, George said, "Do you like that?"

Ray sighed, "Yeah-h-h-h!" They stood and gazed for a moment. Then George said, "And the swimming pool is heated."

In a voice the excitement had pushed down to a whisper, Ray said, "It is?"

Trying not to break the spell, George whispered, "Freeze."

"What was out back?" Pat demanded. He really wanted to know, because he had believed it.

We all agreed that it was the finest and most believable acting Ray had done in the class. He conveyed excitement and joy. The audience felt it because Ray felt it. What made it work? What happened inside Ray that enabled him to create this excitement and joy? We can only speculate, of course, about what happens inside someone. But from our knowledge of Ray, it seemed that he had used some of his own needs and fantasies as a basis for his dramatic creation.

In choosing George to help him and giving him the role of an omnipotent servant, he was trying George out in the kind of role he had in Ray's fantasies. Ray seemed to be hoping that this adult, unlike others, could be trusted and would be able to help him out of his isolation and feelings of worthlessness.

Ray had started their conversation by demanding repeated assurance of his power over the jinni. He tested him further by ordering him back into the pipe, certainly a far less harrowing form of testing than teachers are often put through when they treat embittered students with unaccustomed respect. In wishing for a castle and being convincingly thrilled with it, Ray was externalizing fantasies stemming from his family circumstances. He was one of eleven children. His family lived in close quarters, and Ray shared a small bedroom with three brothers. The father, a low-salaried laborer, frequently got drunk and beat the children. It was natural for Ray to express his fantasies by wishing for spacious housing in which he could have a room to himself. With the view of reality he had acquired from living with a poor family in squalid housing with a drunken father, getting a nice big place to live would have to be a feat of magic. Thus, the jinni.

Ray was able to show this much of himself only after two months of improvisational drama, in which time he came to trust the others in his group somewhat, and after testing George and finding him reliable. Trusting the others freed him to act—to create and project an experience based on something within himself. Perhaps by sharing his fantasy with us he was able to lessen the impact of his unmet needs. He may even have gained some understanding.

In introducing the class to the day's improvisations, George had talked about believing what one is doing and thus making the audience believe it. Within that focus on believability, there are many different ways in which the student can explore and express himself. The way Ray took was wish fulfillment, which for most children is one of the earliest forms of acting.

Another form of dramatic self-expression is reenactment of a painful or pleasant experience. Reenacting a painful experience sometimes helps to lessen the pain, and a more acceptable resolution might arise. Yet another form of expression is role reversal, in which the student plays someone with whom he feels in conflict. He might play a savage parody of his antagonist, or he might act the way he thinks that person—perhaps a parent—ought to be.

These are only a few of the forms of reality testing that come into play in improvisational drama. There usually is no point in telling students what form of dramatic self-expression they have used. It is better to keep the emphasis close to the surface, on believability, relationships with people, and alternative ways of doing things.

In striving for believability, the actor or improvisational drama student draws on his own emotional and cerebral experience. If he must portray a weak person, he must concentrate on times in his life when he has been weak, try to understand what he felt then, and work from there. If he is to create something he has never been—a weak teacher, for example—he might go through his experiences as a student to recall the behavior of a weak teacher. By calling on his own feelings of weakness and his observation of a weak teacher's actions, he might be able to play the role believably.

How do I think? What is the difference between how I think and how an old man thinks? Acting lends itself to this kind of questioning. Drama makes people reach into themselves to find and use the tools they have there. If the student becomes more purposefully introspective and learns to understand his emotions, he has achieved the essence of both acting and improvisational drama.

Artie, a lanky, amiable black, was asked to be a Black Muslim in a conversation with another boy, who was to be nonmilitant. During the conversation, Artie became quite persuasive. Finally, pounding his fist with convincing passion, he said, "Don't you understand, brother, you are *black*! B-L-A-C-K!"

In discussing the improvisation afterwards, a classmate said, "I didn't know you was a militant." Another agreed that it was hard to believe Artie was not speaking for himself. Artie explained that a Black Muslim had talked at length with his father a few days before. Artie had recalled the Muslim's arguments and used them. In doing the improvisation, Artie said he realized that certain aspects of militancy appealed to him, although he was still largely opposed to it. He had avoided thinking about the question of black militancy before, because of his parents' low opinion of it. After acting the part, however, he was better able to examine the pros and cons of militancy, as well as his feelings about race.

STANISLAVSKI'S INFLUENCE

Konstantin Stanislavski, director of the Moscow Art Theater, probably contributed more than any other person to the understanding of what acting is and should be. "Before Stanislavski, drama schools everywhere in the world taught only the physical elements of an actor's training: ballet, fencing, voice, speech, diction. There was no inner acting technique."[1]

Stanislavski's system is based on the belief that to be real, honest, and creative in his work, the actor must clear a path so that his true emotions and creativeness can come forth. "All we can do is learn how not to interfere with the creativeness of nature, or work to prepare the ground, seek out the motives and means whereby even obliquely we can catch hold of these emotional, super-conscious objectives."[2]

Writing about what has come to be called "the method," Sonia Moore says:

Stanislavski knew that an actor's mind, will and emotions—the three forces responsible for our psychological life—must participate in the creation of a live human being on stage. In the evocation of emotions Stanislavski faced a difficult problem. He discovered that there are mechanisms in human beings which are not subordinate to our control. For instance, we cannot at will slow our heart's palpitation or dilate blood vessels as we can close our eyes or raise a hand, nor can an actor who comes on stage with no personal reason for experiencing emotions of fear, compassion, joy or grief command them, because emotional reactions also belong to such uncontrolled mechanisms.

The problem seemed insoluble until, while watching great actors, he observed that though an actor has no real reason to suffer or to rejoice on stage, he begins to have true emotions when he is inspired. This thought brought Stanislavski to the idea that the subconscious—which he had perceived as an uncontrolled complex of emotions—is not altogether unapproachable, and that there must be a kind of key which would intentionally 'turn on' this inner mechanism.[3]

From his belief that a person's psychological and physical actions are related, Stanislavski developed a "method of physical actions" by which actors could establish a connection to real emotions. The actors were trained to concentrate, not on the indicated emotions, but on the actions that would accompany those emotions. As they focused on the actions, Stanislavski believed, the emotions would engender themselves.

Stanislavski's method of physical actions is basic to improvisational drama. The actors are taught to concentrate on the actions they would execute if they were a certain character in a specific situation. From their choice of actions, students begin to learn about themselves.

NURTURING PRIMARY CREATIVITY

Although acting is our fundamental instrument, and our classes are often exciting to watch, the kind of acting we use is different from that used in producing plays. Understanding the psychological distinction between the two kinds of acting is important.

Improvisational acting comes closer to pure primary creativity than does staging a well-rehearsed play, which involves both primary and secondary creativity. In discussing the useful distinction between primary and secondary creativity, we rely heavily on Abraham H. Maslow's *Toward a Psychology of Being.*[4]

Maslow describes primary creativity as requiring total acceptance of whatever comes from within the self. "It can come only if a person's depths are available to him, only if he is not afraid of his primary thought processes." Primary creativity is spontaneous, intuitive, daring, and imaginative. It "is best exemplified by the improvisation, as in jazz or in childlike paintings, rather than by the work of art designated as 'great.'"

When the secondary processes take over, as in a professional dramatic production, "The voluntary regression into our depths is now terminated, the necessary passivity and receptivity of inspiration or of peak-experience must now give way to activity, control, and hard work." Secondary creativity requires training, rigorous criticism, and reality testing. According to Maslow, the kind of creativity that uses both primary and secondary processes is needed in most professional creative work; the great works of art, philosophy, and science come from this integrated creativity.

But the primary thought processes are not valuable *only* because they provide the material that can be shaped into pragmatic products through secondary processes. Much of the joy of human life springs from primary processes. In discussing the suppression of primary thought and its devastating effect on the potential of human beings, Maslow writes:

> The normal adjustment of the average, common sense, well-adjusted man implies a continued successful rejection of much of the depths of human nature, both conative and cognitive. To adjust well to the world of reality means a splitting of the person. It means that the person turns his back on much in himself because it is dangerous. But it is now clear that by so doing, he loses a great deal too, for these depths are also the source of all his joys, his ability to play, to love, to laugh, and, most important for us, to be creative. By protecting himself against the hell within himself, he also cuts himself off from the heaven within. In the extreme instance, we have the obsessional person, flat, tight, rigid, frozen, controlled, cautious, who can't laugh or play or love, or be silly or trusting or childish. His imagination, his intuitions, his softness, his emotionality tend to be strangulated or distorted.

Primary processes are turned away from, forgotten, or suppressed, Maslow writes, "as we have to adjust to a harsh reality which demands a purposeful and pragmatic striving rather than revery, poetry, play." He adds,

> I expect that education processes, which are known to do rather little for relieving repression of 'instinct,' can do much to accept and integrate the primary processes into conscious and preconscious life. Education in art, poetry, dancing, can in principle do much in this direction.

We discuss primary creativity here because we want to distinguish clearly between our use of acting as an educational instrument and the use that is made of acting in entertaining and edifying audiences. This is important, because the climate and style of work that we like to create in a class are based on our concern with primary processes, not with the secondary creativity needed to polish a theatrical work.

Any class emphasizing the nurture of primary creativity should be free of reproach. There should be no rigorous criticism or censorship of what the participants express. Reproach, censorship, moralizing, and criticism make students put self-defense before self-discovery. In a repressive or hypercritical climate, caution and control replace daring and freedom.

The class should be as free as possible from suggestions by the teacher. Students who are eager to please will try quite hard to figure out what the teacher wants. Although they do not think of deceiving the teacher, they might deceive themselves, by trumping up the "right" emotion. On the other hand, if a student has figured out what the teacher wants but cannot produce the appropriate feeling, he may feel that he is a failure because he has disappointed the teacher.

The teacher should avoid giving authoritarian advice. Even if such advice is correct, timely, and nonthreatening, by giving his students insights they have not yet discovered, the teacher may be inviting them to give up the struggle for mature independence.

Although acting is the fundamental instrument of improvisational drama, a class that comes reasonably close to the openness just described is quite different from a theatrical acting class. It is tragic that this openness alone also makes the class unlike anything most students have experienced in a school.

In his excellent theoretical work, *Neurotic Distortion of the Creative Process,* Lawrence S. Kubie writes,

it has been the traditionally accepted role of the school to impose even stronger taboos on self-knowledge than are generated at home, thus reinforcing and reproducing in the classroom the very limitations on self-awareness which characterize our adult culture. Thus what passes for Education strengthens that all-too-human tendency to shrink from the facing of painful facts, which the child brings to school from his nursery.

   . . . most schools still exploit competitively the hostilities and the sibling rivalries which arise automatically in every nursery. Almost never are these resolved or illuminated in the classroom with insight, grace, or compassion.

   . . . the immediate and the remote effects of these internal and external sources of conflict upon each child and adult will depend *not* upon the fact that these struggles occur, but upon the level on which they are waged, i.e., whether this level is preponderantly conscious, preconscious, or unconscious. Therefore we can justly challenge our schools to see what they can do to make sure that these battles will be fought out on conscious and preconscious levels. It would seem to be an essential ingredient of any truly educational experience to enable each child to face in himself those painful conflicts from which he shrinks but which shape his character.[5]

Nearly everyone who teaches, no matter how well intentioned and versed in theory, finds himself itching to push students out of primary processes and into striving for productive perfection. Virtually all of us have undergone extensive conditioning that makes it difficult for us to trust children (or each other) to start where they are and develop in ways that they choose. We can hardly wait to start "constructively" telling them how to do it "better." This probably is even harder to avoid in teaching writing than in teaching art, improvisational drama, or other subjects that conformists in education tell us are "frills" anyhow.

We might remind ourselves that when people are unable to liberate their primary processes, their secondary processes have less original material to work with. When a person's primary processes are temporarily freed through any expressive medium they are more likely to be available to him for other uses.

People who are both primarily and secondarily creative in one medium or activity are very likely to show the spark of primary creativity in other fields. For example, we know an accomplished painter who also dabbles occasionally in writing, photography, dancing, acting, music, or anything else that catches his fancy. Judged by professional standards, his results are laughable, but the spontaneous, daring, imaginative spark is usually there. His primary processes usually flow freely, but only in painting has he put in the years of training and hard work that enable him to mold his creative outpourings into products that people will pay money for. Without access to the riches inside himself, however, no amount of training or hard work would have made him a creative painter.

The constructive teaching we aim for requires knowing each student well enough to know when and how we should help him begin to develop secondary skills. When the climate and structure of an improvisational drama class are sufficiently open, safe, accepting, and stimulating, the students can be spontaneous and daring in responding to unexpected challenges. Though never eliminated, stereotyped responses will appear less and less frequently. The improvisational drama class can be a part of the kind of educational process Kubie called for when he wrote:

Maturity requires the capacity to change, to become different, to react in varied and unanticipated ways. All of these words describe different facets of this same human need: and none of it is attainable as long as the human spirit remains imprisoned in its masked neuroses. This is the ultimate challenge to the value of any educational process in any culture.[6]

FOOTNOTES

1. Sonia Moore, *The Stanislavski System* (New York: Viking Press, 1965), p. 10.

2. Konstantin Stanislavski, *Creating a Role* (New York: Theater Arts Books, 1961), p. 52.

3. Moore, *Stanislavski System,* pp. 12-13.

4. Abraham H. Maslow, *Toward a Psychology of Being* (New York: D. Van Nostrand Co., 1962), pp. 133-35.

5. Lawrence S. Kubie, *Neurotic Distortion of the Creative Process* (New York: Noonday Press, 1961), pp. 120-21.

6. Ibid., p. 136.

Four:
GETTING
STARTED

"It seems like magic!"

We've heard those words many times from people who watch an improvisational drama class that has been working together for a few weeks. Unfortunately, it is not magic. The teacher has to know what he is doing to bring a class to the point where the students move and express themselves freely without breaking down the classroom walls.

There are principles for starting a class right. Many of these principles are fundamentally the same for improvisational drama as for any other course: How can the teacher get students involved, create a safe and stimulating climate, establish order without rigidity, and help students safely through the early phases of development?

PHYSICAL SETTING

Educators who watch our classes often have the feeling that they take place in a strange, elaborate setting. They seem surprised when they analyze the setting and realize how simple and easy to duplicate it is. We have used a variety of environments, setting them up quickly in such places as a room above a store or a faculty room. There are a few conditions we always include.

1. The room is darkened, with heavy window coverings for daytime. For this, a large roll of opaque black plastic can be bought from a hardware store for a few dollars. A small spotlight is hung over the center of the area to be used as a stage. For the spotlight, we sometimes use a half-gallon can wrapped in black art paper with a light bulb in the center. An extension cord is taped to the ceiling and brought over to the wall, so that it can be dropped down the side and does not interfere with movement on the stage.

2. Large cushions or chairs are arranged around part of the stage area. Sometimes they are in a semicircle, forming a half-moon with a wall as the straight line. Or the stage area can be in a corner of the room, with the cushions or chairs in two straight lines, at right angles to each other and to the walls, forming a square stage. We prefer to use large cushions for seating, but if some of the participants are old enough to have lost their limberness, we use chairs.

3. The only other equipment needed for every class is a record player and a handful of records covering a variety of moods and beats, as well as records selected especially for each class.

When the group has more than twenty-two members, we use one of two arrangements. If we are running a workshop with only one or two sessions, the participants are seated in an oval or circle. If it is to be a longer course, we use the half-moon, but with two semicircles of seats, one behind the other. The two rows alternate from one session to the next between front and back. Most of the activities are done only by those in the front row. The entire group takes part in discussions.

The illusory world of our classroom helps participants suspend conventional ways of behavior and sustain involvement. A suitable environment for improvisational drama will differ from class to class. Once established, however, this environment should not be changed very often. When people are dealing very specifically with difficult matters they must be relaxed about everything else. If students come to expect their drama class to be held in a semidark room with cushions to sit on, their cultivated feelings of security could vanish in different surroundings.

TEACHER

From the moment the students enter the room, the teacher should be strong and confident, as well as warm and accepting. If students sense fear in the teacher, they may be afraid to try new things and eventually open themselves up.

The teacher should have his class planned, with some alternatives. He should be alert and flexible enough to alter his plans if the students give cues that call for it, but he should understand his objectives clearly enough to stick with them even in altering his plans. The teacher should keep his notes on what he wants to do in

the class in some unobtrusive place. They are there only for emergen-
cies: he should memorize his plans so the class can flow naturally
without his calling attention to the previous planning by consulting
notes.

Above all, the teacher should put vitality and meaning into everything he does. He should not drag around on the stage. He should not
even go on the stage without a reason. John Dewey and many other
educators have said that what students learn from observing and
being around the teacher is as important as anything in their school
experience. The teacher's vitality and sincerity are communicable to
students, but if the teacher is sluggish or uninvolved, the class
languishes under a wet blanket.

Like an athlete, musician, or anyone else who must be ready to go
at a given time, the teacher should develop his own routines for
getting into the mood before class. One of our teachers usually put
on a rock record and danced just before his first class of the day.
Others have developed a series of exercises to get the blood flowing.
There might be times when a teacher needs to relax and meditate
quietly on what he is about to do.

Most teachers approach the first improvisational drama class they
teach with the trepidation of an actor on opening night. Sometimes
the stage fright is so intense that the teacher thinks he cannot go
through with it. But he can, of course, and once he gets the group
and himself moving, he is all right.

PARALLEL FORMATS

As we teach improvisational drama, the format of each day's class
tends to recapitulate the progression of the entire course. The course
progresses from emphasis on physical freeing in the early lessons to
emphases on concentration, believability, and, finally, relationships.
Even after the group has reached the relationships stage, daily classes
usually begin with warm-ups that emphasize physical freeing and
concentration. These help prepare the students for the rest of the
class in which believability and relationships are emphasized.

FIRST DAY

Whether they are eleven-year-olds, high school students, or adults,
students who have never experienced anything like improvisational
drama before are filled with ambivalence. A record is playing as they

enter the room, and they are attracted by the excitement of the music and mystery. But many still yearn for the secure ennui they have been conditioned to expect in much of their school experience. Therefore, on the first day the teacher should play it safe. The class should be intriguing and pleasurable, but not overpowering or frightening. It is like another world—a world of fantasy and illusion—and that is enough strangeness.

After greeting the students warmly and inviting them to take seats, we start the first activity. We do not use preliminary discussions with any group, whether we are starting a full course or a one-shot three-hour session with adults. Starting with verbal rationalization would contradict what we want to accomplish. As Karel Capek wrote, "If dogs could talk, perhaps we'd find it just as hard to get along with them as we do with people." To help people start our courses without being hamstrung by their verbal defenses, we begin with a minimum of talking by the teacher and virtually none by the students.

Later sessions can start with uninhibited dancing, but the first few should begin in a controlled fashion to ease anxiety. The teacher should not ask the students to do anything frightening or make more than minimal decisions about what they will do. The activity that starts the first class might be a pantomime demonstration by the teacher, or a rhythm activity in which both students and teacher participate.

George started one first class by putting on a record of circus music and sounds. He drew the kids into a small circle around the lighted spot on the floor. In the center, in a striped T-shirt, he reacted to the record with mimes of a wire walker, a ringmaster, and a strongman. The kids watched with wide-eyed intensity until they broke up laughing at a clown routine.

By starting in this way, George was using himself as a model. He demonstrated physical freedom, concentration, and believability, which would be three of the four emphases as the course progressed. He put everything he had into the performance, displaying the kind of daring and commitment that he would be calling on the kids to develop in themselves. The kids believed that he believed in what he was doing, which later would help them to believe in themselves. This kind of start is especially appropriate for a class of pubescent boys who have a strong need for models as they make their adolescent personality transitions.

When the students are adults or in their late teens, we start with an activity in which the teacher calls on the students to join him. This kind of beginning is suitable to any age, and might be preferable for a teacher who is trying improvisational drama for the first time. Three sample exercises follow. Because the students are seated in these exercises, the movements are less threatening and the students are more willing to get involved.

1. *Clapping*. The teacher starts a record, takes his seat with the students, and starts to clap the beat. The students probably will take it up. If not, he genially calls to them to join in. He then calls out instructions such as: "Fingers" (and snaps his fingers), "on the off beat," "be completely unmusical—no beat at all." He might have them double the beat or slow it down. The exercise ends when the teacher springs to his feet and starts the next activity.

2. *Isolated Body Movements, Seated, with Music*. With the students seated, the teacher starts a record and takes his seat. "Hands," he calls, clapping to the music. The teacher and students tap the floor and otherwise move their hands freely to the music. "Only the hands. Make them free!" the teacher might call.

Then, in turn, the teacher calls "arms, head, shoulders, chest." For each one, he calls any words of encouragement that seem to be needed, such as: "Do something different! Make it BIG! Only the head. Bigger. Move big." When they have moved their chests for a minute, he calls: "Put it all together."

As students become comfortable with the class, this same exercise can be done standing. After chests comes hips and then feet. And there they are—dancing.

3. *Isolated Body Movements, Seated, without Music*. This exercise can follow either clapping or isolated body movements with music. Begin as in the previous exercise, but without music, moving the hands, arms, head, shoulders, and then chest in isolation. Then move all of the parts together. Next, the teacher instructs the class to express a variety of emotions with the bodily parts in isolation—hands, arms, head, shoulders, chest, and then all together. The teacher calls out such words as *fear, happiness, anger, love,* and *freedom* for them to express.

Next, the teacher instructs:

"Pick up something sticky. It's right there on the floor in front of you, and you have to pick it up."

"Pick up something you like. Be specific. Think of a specific thing you like. How does it feel?"

"Now! There is something you're afraid of on the floor in front of you. You fear it greatly. But you have to pick it up. Pick it up and hold it."

The warm-ups over, a change of record can denote a different mood for the next part of the class. For the middle part of the first class, we usually put the emphasis on thinking, not on acting. We want the students to start realizing that acting involves thinking, and we want acting to start being personally meaningful for them.

For one first class, George put a heavy symphony on the record player and said slowly, "Stare at the center of the circle. Think about this, and later you might have a chance to show us. It's the last day of school. You have failed everything. You were not expected to fail anything. You have to take your report card home. How do you feel? Think about how you would feel."

This think-first-and-act-later kind of assignment is well suited for the group's first improvisation. The specific assignment—concentrating on how it feels to be a failure—was appropriate to that group of boys, most of whom start a school year dominated by fears of failure. Of this group, only a few of the boys were given a chance to demonstrate their thoughts on the subject in an improvisation, but all of them were expected to concentrate on the assignment as if they might be chosen.

After a pause, George stepped decisively toward one of the boys, extended a hand to him, helped him to his feet, and guided him to the center. He repeated that it was the last day of school and that the boy had failed everything. "You must stay in the center until I bring you out of the center," George said. He gives this instruction several times in each of the first few classes, until it becomes a natural part of the structure.

Students do not stop an improvisation when they choose to stop. The teacher stops the improvisation when, for any of a number of reasons, he decides to stop it. Often, especially in these early sessions, the students come up with what are largely stereotyped responses to a task. For instance, when told that he has failed everything in school, a student might go through the motions of opening a report card, doing a goggle-eyed double take, and then slouching around with an "aw, shucks" look. At this point, he might glance at the teacher, or he might forget his instructions and go to his seat. His programming has run out, and he is ready to knock off. In this case, the teacher says, "Continue. Don't stop until I tell you to. You must stay in the center until I bring you out of the center."

Since he has to continue the improvisation with his stereotyped responses used up, the actor might start now to express something, to imagine how he would actually react to this failure: by kicking and cursing, becoming passively sullen and depressed, bursting into tears, or whatever.

Of course, the task is not difficult. The student can react by just standing there, or by sitting on the floor. The task has caused them to go on the stage, and perhaps to call on something within to show how they have felt in the past or how they might feel in a given situation.

On this first day of class, George gave six of these think-and-then-do assignments. A few boys were chosen to improvise each one. The second task was, "It is a day last summer. A beautiful day. You really had a great time on this particular day. Think about that day."

Ray was the third boy to be placed in the center for this task. He did nothing. It appeared that he might be the first to fail at his task. George stepped into the improvisation with him, like an actor making an entrance. He sat down and motioned the boy to sit opposite him. Then George dealt an imaginary deck of cards. The uncertainty and fear left Ray's face as he deftly picked up the cards. This was something he knew. As the game progressed, George repeatedly tried to peek at Ray's hand. Ray lost patience and jumped to his feet. George stood up, too, and a pantomime quarrel ensued.

Suddenly George stepped back and threw his hands in the air with a smile. The spell was broken. George shook Ray's hand and guided him to his seat, then changed the record as he gave instructions for the next task: "You're in a school yard. You were in a fight. Everybody's looking, and you lost. Everybody's looking, even the girls. And you lost. How you gonna feel. Show us."

As they did this exercise, it was apparent that already the students were becoming more involved. The aura was starting to grow.

The other assignments for that class:

"It's eleven o'clock at night, and you're not on your own turf. You're on somebody else's turf, and you see a bunch of guys coming toward you."

"It's a rainy day. A Saturday. You're not going to school."

"You're sitting in a classroom. You don't like that teacher. The teacher bugs you. Try to picture a teacher you don't like. Picture yourself sitting in the teacher's class. How do you feel? Show us."

Some of these assignments can be used again six or seven weeks later, and it is interesting to see how much more the students are able to put into them.

After the last improvisation, George started a record and briskly brought the group together in a circle on their knees.

"Think of some way to keep time to the music. Now change it. Now change again and don't use your hands."

Following George's lead, they leaned forward, placed their hands in the light, and drummed on the floor in time to the music.

"Just move one finger," George laughed. "Now, press down on the floor. Press hard. Harder! C'mon, we gotta push that floor *down* there, baby!"

As each strained the palms of both hands against the floor, George called, "Up on your knees."

Upright on their knees, they swayed happily to the jazz beat until George jumped up, snapped on the light, and said:

"Thank you. We'll see you tomorrow."

They were initiated.

TIMING THE CLASS

Timing is something a teacher learns through experience. While becoming acquainted with the techniques of improvisational drama, he should be careful to not run out of time before taking the group through a suitable ending.

The beginning teacher's lesson plan for the first day may go like this:

1. *Warm-ups.* Start with the isolated body movements, seated, with music described above. Then skip to the last part of isolated body movements, seated, without music—the part in which the students express emotions with parts of the body—and continue through picking things up from the floor.

2. *Middle.* Continue with a handful of improvisations that all of the students will think about but only a few will do. Examples: "It's a beautiful day last summer." "You're sitting in a classroom and you don't like that teacher."

3. *Ending.* Finish with the ending just described, done by the students on their knees.

The teacher needs to remember not to rush anything, and to leave five minutes at the end for the ending. If the group has done only the first improvisation when the class is five minutes from its end, the teacher should move on to the planned ending.

TO CONTINUE

If the teacher can gain the group's trust and cooperation in the first few days, the course will progress better throughout the semester.

On the second day, we usually repeat the same warm-ups and ending we used on the first day, except that we have the students standing in a circle instead of sitting or kneeling. By the time they are moving everything, including hips and legs, they are more or less dancing. But we do not use the word *dance* until after the students use it. In a discussion one day, Pat grumbled that he was embarrassed about dancing (which he later came to love) and could not do it. "But you don't have to call it dancing," another boy said. That seemed to make a difference, and it made even more of a difference to many of the adults with whom we have worked.

It is usually wise for the teacher to do the warm-ups along with the students for the first few weeks. This helps the students to be less self-conscious.

From the very beginning of a course, our teachers do not allow applause. We do not mention applause before it actually occurs, but the first time it happens, and on any subsequent occasions, the teacher says, "We don't applaud in here. We're all worthy of applause in this class." The teacher should then compliment the actors so they will know that he is not disagreeing with the applause. We think that if the teacher warned against applause before it happened, he might be fostering a tacit feeling of competition. Always, the teacher is fully interested in and accepting of everything the students do.

INVOLVEMENT, NOT PUNISHMENT

A school should give kids plenty of opportunities for horseplay. But in something like improvisational drama, where a group of people works together for a creative end, serious involvement is required. If there is adequate involvement, there are no discipline problems. The only discipline needed is the discipline of the activity itself.

If concentration lags enough that the activities lose force, the teacher need say nothing about it. Instead he should act quickly to help the students regain their concentration. If the class seems phlegmatic, for example, the teacher might stride briskly back and forth in front of them, demonstrating as he says, "Make fists of your hands. Pulse your hands. Squeeze. Relax. Squeeze. Relax. Keep pulsing them. Now, tense the muscles in your body. Tense all of your muscles. Strain! Relax." Then: "Get your concentration back and let's go!" he says cheerfully as he swings into a continuation of the class.

When the noise level is too high, relaxation techniques are called for. This can be as simple as, "Everybody take a deep breath. Deep breath. Hold it . . . let it out!" Or the class might need a full-fledged relaxation series, as described in chapter five. This approach implicitly communicates that the teacher thinks the students want to be involved, and he is helping them to regain their involvement. There is no implication that the kids have been bad or wanted to be bad. No student is put down. This approach to maintaining involvement works in virtually any course.

The instruction "freeze" is a big help. Unlike "halt" or "stoppit," "freeze" is an action instruction. That is important, because the moment one says "stop," the student may cut off, losing his vitality and involvement. "Freeze" is a positive instruction that says, "Maintain it without moving." The teacher might follow "freeze" with an instruction such as, "Don't move a muscle. Maintain."

It usually is not taken as a prohibition. In fact, many kids take pride in freezing every muscle precisely as it was when they heard "freeze." In our experience, every time a kid has started to get out of hand, "freeze" has stopped him and held him until he could be given other instructions or have his task clarified.

Five:
WARM-UPS

We usually go about designing one day's class something like this:

1. By reviewing what has happened and thinking about the people in the group, we determine what we want to explore in the class. This becomes an open-ended theme.

2. We plan what we will do in the middle or main part of the class to make it more likely that what we want to happen will indeed come about. This plan should include some alternatives.

3. We design a beginning for the class, with some alternatives, to set the desired mood and tone and prepare the group for the middle. We call our beginnings "warm-ups."

4. We design an ending for the class.

5. We go over the plan to be sure that it is well orchestrated, that each part grows smoothly and meaningfully into the text.

Having made his plan and committed it to memory, the teacher rarely follows it. Making the plan is part of the process of preparing himself to be responsive and helpful to students in the class. (See chapter thirteen.)

This chapter is about using warm-ups to begin classes in ways that will lead to productive middles and ends. All teachers face this challenge, and teachers in many fields have used our warm-up techniques and approaches effectively in starting their classes.

If the middle of the class requires quiet concentration, the beginning should focus on getting the students to concentrate. If the intended experience requires great energy and vitality, then warm-ups might be planned to stimulate the students' bodies, senses, and imaginations. The uses of warm-ups are unlimited. For a group with some verbally inhibited members, we might include verbal exercises in the warm-ups.

In thinking about one of his groups, George decided that the purpose of the next one-hour session would be to get the students to think about their lives and how they would like to change. For the middle, he decided to say, "If you could go back to any age you wanted and change something about your life, what age would you go back to, and how would you change your life? Think about this, and when I bring you to the center of the stage, act it out. What would you do physically? What would your actions be? You may talk or not talk, as you please." He would give the class a few minutes to think, and then bring a student to the center of the stage. Each student would get a chance to explore this experience alone on the stage.

The next step in planning was to come up with a beginning that would enable students to benefit from that middle. Here is how the class actually started:

Soft music played as the students entered the darkened room. George asked them to sit and listen quietly to the music. As soon as the entire class of twelve people, mostly graduate students, was there, George stepped into the spotlight on center stage and asked them to lie on their backs with only their heads on the pillows. He guided them to relaxation by isolating single parts of the body and letting go of each until it felt relaxed.

"Begin with your feet and ankles. Let them go." Then we worked upward, taking time to concentrate on each part of the body. Legs, stomach, chest and arms, neck and head. Finally, we concentrated on the face, telling the students that their lower jaws should drop open. "The eyes, though closed, should feel as though they are almost opening of their own accord. The skin should feel as though it is being pulled into the ground."

As the students lay there, we began breath control, which involves inhaling through the nose until the stomach and chest are fully expanded. Then the air is forced out through the mouth. The students breathe at a signal from the teacher. After inhaling and exhaling in unison a few times, the students are told to pace their breathing themselves.

The students had been concentrating on specifics: relaxing parts of their bodies and breathing. They were not concentrating simply on concentration, which usually produces only daydreaming or fantasizing.

Now that they were concentrating, George told the students, who were still controlling their breathing, "Think back to when you were younger. Think back as far as you can possibly remember. See yourself. What did you look like? How did you dress? How did you move and speak?"

At this point, we had begun to shift the area of concentration and were ready for the transition to the next part of the warm-ups. We wanted to get the students to think concretely about their lives. We began by having them crawl from their pillows onto the stage. As they lay on the stage with their eyes closed, George said, "Think about the important things that have happened to you during your lifetime." He gave them time to think about this. "Now, through pantomime, trace your life from birth to this moment, keeping your eyes closed. Trace your life from the very beginning to the present."

After about ten minutes, even if many have not progressed to the present, the teacher usually stops the pantomime.

"Freeze. Return to your cushions."

It is not important that the students finish this exercise. What is important is that they have been thinking about their lives and have been seeing the past.

Warm-ups can be regarded as freeing from such irrelevancies as physical and mental tension, the lethargic defense, inhibition, distraction, self-consciousness, and fear. This group, in preparing to face a potentially threatening situation, had begun in a serene climate. They were put through experiences in relaxing and concentrating. When they all pantomimed their biographies together with eyes shut, they had the reassurance of knowing that everyone else was doing the same thing at the same time and that their classmates were not looking at them. Keeping their eyes shut also helped them concentrate within themselves and be more honest. They had stripped away many of the irrelevancies.

After the class, the students agreed that the experience had been a powerful, provocative one for them. They talked not only of the lone improvisations, but also of the blind, group pantomimes that were part of the warm-ups. Often, warm-ups are as meaningful as anything in the class, and the term we use for them should not give the impression that their only value is to prepare people for the rest of the class.

Beginnings are important. Playwrights, filmmakers, and other artists working in temporal media know that their beginnings have to hook the viewer and prepare him for what is to come. The teacher's temporal challenge is especially complex; he has a new beginning every day at the start of each class.

Urban teachers are often advised that they should always have something written on the chalkboard before students enter the classroom. The students are to sit down and start copying from the board as soon as they come in. This practice is based on the correct belief that urban children—many of whom have a high level of anxiety—feel more secure in a class with a clear structure and substantial routine. Copying from the chalkboard is a sound way to begin a class, if you want to prepare students to be passively docile. Not all teachers are on such firm ground. Some have no beginning at all: the bell rings and suddenly they are "teaching," as if there had been no respite from yesterday's class.

A class, in improvisational drama or anything else, should have a consistent structure. If most of the students come from chaotic backgrounds, as is often true of inner-city schools, there should be some routine. (A routine does not have to be boring.) What we want teachers to see is that the structuring activities should contribute to the fulfillment of the purpose of the class.

ENERGIZING THE GROUP

For many classes, the students need to be vital and physically free. Below is a sample warm-up for energizing a class.

Lively jazz or rock surges through the room as the students enter. When the last student is seated, the teacher closes the door, takes his seat, and claps to the music. The students pick it up, and after about half a minute the teacher bounds to the center and says, "Everybody up! Around me in a circle!"

With the music still blasting, they warm up with isolated body movements. Head, arms, shoulders, hips, legs. "Put it all together and move to that music!"

Through physical example and verbal encouragement, the teacher emphasizes big movements. The people fairly fly apart on the driving currents of music. As they move, the teacher calls out, "The ground is on fire. You're got to continue to move, but the ground is on fire." After a few minutes, this one is really getting wild. Before chaos ensues, the teacher calls, "Freeze," and lifts the needle from the record.

Speaking slowly and deliberately in the stunning silence, he says, "Hold it. Don't move. Ver-r-r-ry slowly, get small. Slowly get small."

As the people curl into knots on the floor: "Strain as you're getting smaller. Tighten all the muscles. Get small as you tighten." Even after they are as small as they can possibly get, the teacher urges, "Smaller. Smaller."

Then, "Slo-o-o-owly, get big!" While directing the group to get ever bigger, the teacher starts a record of a flowing melody. When the people are very big, up on their toes: "The wind is blowing gently. Become a leaf in that wind. That gentle wind is blowing you about."

"The wind is getting stronger. A little bit stronger." Gradually, the teacher's voice takes on urgency as the wind continues to gain strength. When the people are swirling about the room with abandon, bumping into the walls and each other: "Freeze."

"You're standing in deep mud. It's really deep mud. You have to walk." As the teacher plods about with the group, he scoops up a glob of mud and slops it in someone's face. Gleefully, he cries, "Let's cover each other with mud! Mud all over everybody! Cover everybody with mud."

When they have clodded each other lustily, the teacher says, "It's starting to rain. Rain! Wash the mud off. Wash it off completely. The mud's off. It's gone. And it's still raining. Have fun in the rain. Really have fun." After a few minutes: "Freeze, and to your seats."

In this exercise, the students go from the high degree of control in the isolated body movements to the very free instruction, "Have fun in the rain." Some might have their fun with other people; some might walk about by themselves; others might just sit on the floor. In any case, now they are energized and ready to move.

WHEN STUDENTS ARE TOO EXCITED

Suppose the students are too excited when they enter. The tasks for the middle of the class will require purposeful concentration, but the kids are horsing around, teasing each other, and giggling. This calls for warm-ups that minimize interaction.

The teacher, standing at center stage, says, "On your backs, with your feet pointing toward me. Take a deep breath. Hold it. Let it out very slowly. Take another deep breath. Take in a little more. A little more. Very slowly—slower—let it out. Slower."

After a few repeats, "Suck your stomach in. Pull it in until it touches your backbone. More. More. More. Relax it!"

This can be repeated, then done the opposite way once or twice: "Push your stomachs out."

Next, "Point your toes toward me. Harder. Harder. Harder!" When they are feeling the pain: "Let it go!"

"Don't move your head, but look to the right. Move only your eyes. *Hard* to the right. Harder. Let it go!"

Repeat to the left.

Then, "Don't move anything, but look at the ceiling. Make your eyes touch the ceiling. Get your eyes out of your head and make them touch the ceiling. Harder. Push them out. Harder. Let it go."

"The ground is a magnet. It's pulling you down. You're being pulled into the ground. Resist it! Resist it harder. Really fight it! It's pulling you harder, but you've got to get up! You've got to get up, but it's pulling you down." The teacher's voice becomes agonized; so do the students' grunts. "You've got to get up, but it won't let you! It's pulling you very hard, but *you can make it*. Fight it. You can make it. Help others make it. Help them. Pull. Pull."

This warm-up has taken the students into themselves in concentrated fashion. Now, they return to interacting with each other—but this time purposefully.

As they help each other up, the teacher gets a record ready to go. When they are all on their feet, the teacher says "freeze" and immediately the music is going.

"Find somebody and help him move to the music."

The teacher does not say how to help, except, "Help them to move bigger."

"Find somebody else; help him to move."

From concentrating within themselves, they have moved to concentrating on someone else.

After several switches: "Freeze, and to your seats."

The snowman is an effective warm-up device for helping students become serene and open. They start out being snowmen, with enough time to feel hard and cold. Then the hot sun beats down on them, and they slowly melt into puddles of water. Then they slowly evaporate and become clouds, gently drifting about.

ADAPTING TO EXISTING MOODS

Usually, the teacher cannot know in advance the mood his students will be in. Who knows what happened in the hall or in their previous class, or how their lunches agreed with them?

The teacher should always have some alternative warm-ups ready for use.

If plans call for the students to be vital and lively, but the students come banging in so high the room won't hold them, a relaxation exercise might be in order. Conversely, even if a quiet, relaxed approach is needed, the group might still be so sluggish and dull that stimulating warm-ups are needed. To impose relaxation exercises on an already phlegmatic class would be foolish.

The teacher can also pick up cues while the warm-ups are going on. During one warm-up session, the boys were instructed first to be very hot, and then freezing. As the assurances that they were freezing continued, the boys clumped together on the floor to get warm. But Mack, an awkward twelve-year-old, shivered by himself a bit to one side of the crowd. Mack seemed relieved, though, when another boy grabbed him and hauled him into the clump.

George noticed this, and reminded himself to give Mack opportunities to overcome his isolation and to feel close to someone else.

VERBAL WARM-UPS

When we have a group in which some of the people talk inaudibly, stammer, or otherwise manifest verbal inhibitions, we sometimes include verbal warm-ups in getting the classes started.

Some of these verbal exercises require quick thinking, as when the teacher calls out words and the students shout a word that means the opposite. But the main value of verbal warm-up activities is the loosening, vitalizing effect of speaking up quickly and forcibly, before fear or internal censorship can block thought or reduce the voice to a whisper.

In doing verbal warm-ups, it is important for the teacher to emphasize making the voice *big*. Behavior therapists and sales managers know the benefits to the inhibited person of simply increasing the force of his voice.

The following are verbal warm-ups that have been effective in our classes:

1. *Mini-Interviews.* In this verbal exercise, the people are in a circle, either seated or standing. The teacher has a microphone, which need not be plugged in. "I'm going to ask a question," the teacher says. "When I stick this microphone in front of your face, you have to give an answer."

Speaking forcibly is emphasized. If someone mumbles, the teacher continues to hold the microphone in front of him and says something like, "We didn't hear you."

Questions can be almost anything that can be answered in a word or two. Generally, the early questions should be pleasurable ice-breakers, such as "What is your favorite make of car?" Next come questions that permit either a superficial answer or self-probing, such as "Name something you're afraid of." (Someone who does not care to reveal much of himself might honestly answer, "alligators.") If the group has been together long enough, the later questions can be on topics relevant to the group and the people in it. "Do you think Robby is with it today?"

2. *Shouting Match.* Two lines of people face each other from opposite sides of the stage. Each has a partner in the opposite line. At "go," all the people in one line simultaneously tell their partners something they've been instructed to tell, such as a joke or a favorite hobby or television show. The object is to shout loud enough to communicate despite the competition from other shouters. The lines alternate at being the shouters.

3. *Timed Talks.* The people are placed in groups of two, three, or four. They are given short periods of time, from ten seconds to two minutes, to tell each other something specified by the teacher. For example,

You have thirty seconds to tell your partner two things that you feel could make him a better person.

You have ten seconds to tell each other what friendship means.

You have ten seconds to tell the other person something you admire about him.

USING WARM-UPS IN REGULAR CLASSES

Teachers who have taken our improvisational drama course find that warm-ups are the first thing they want to use in teaching their regular subjects. Warm-ups are useful and easily adaptable.

A Philadelphia public school teacher who used warm-ups to help his predominantly poor and black students start the day in their home room told us his results were excellent. He found his students better able to focus on their academic classes. They also had more positive feelings about home room. On days when the warm-ups were skipped, the students found it harder to settle down; they wanted and expected the warm-ups. Home room was the only time they got together, and the warm-up structure gave them a sort of ritual they could share. As the home room students began to understand the structuring of the warm-ups, they participated enthusiastically in planning and leading them.

Six:

PHYSICAL FREEING

The soul does not like to be without its body, because without the body it cannot feel or do anything; therefore build a figure in such a way that its pose tells what is in the soul of it.
—Leonardo da Vinci

Against the jolting rhythms of the "West Side Story" overture, George cried, "You've gotta be a gang leader. How are you gonna do it? Think about it. How are you gonna make that shadow be a gang leader? Not just a member of a gang, but a gang leader."

Using the gang experience familiar to all of them, each boy expressed his notion of himself as a leader. The beam of a slide projector cast their shadows on a wall.

Charles, a small, sullen black boy, went first. He was hesitant and timorous, unable to imagine himself as a leader at all. Shaking his head in disbelief, Chet raised his hand to go next. Instead, George called on tiny, pugnacious Pat.

Chest and chin puffed out, Pat swaggered about on the balls of his feet to look taller. With jerky motions, he signaled Wilt, Doug, and Ray to join him as his followers.

When Pat's turn was over, George said, "All right, Chet, you try it." Chet, who was already a street corner veteran, played it cool and slinky. Unlike Charles and Pat, he seemed to be having fun.

After some other students had done their interpretations, the boys discussed which ones had looked most like real gang leaders. Generally, they rated Chet the highest and Pat the lowest. Pat was surprised, since he had acted as tough as he possibly could.

During the first week of the class, Pat complained about moving to music, which he insisted was dancing and therefore sissy stuff. Everything he did made it clear that to him the important thing was to be callous and brave in a swaggering, physical way.

During the second week, Pat's personal creed began to undergo a substantial change. It seemed to us that the change, which appeared as a kind of philosophical or emotional growth, was made possible partly by the physical freeing activity of the class. Pat had been quite excited by a fencing drill, done without foils, in the class. In shadow play he became confident enough to be imaginative in his movements.

One day in the second week, the class went through an advanced physical freeing activity that would have been too threatening to use in the first few days. George played records ranging from African drums to Tchaikovsky and placed students alone on the stage with instructions simply to "react to the music."

Pat was the second student to go on the stage. His music was a selection from "The Nutcracker." Without hesitation or self-consciousness he put his hands above his head and daintily swirled about the stage like a ballerina.

As George shook Pat's hand, another boy exclaimed, "That took guts!" In discussion, the boys were filled with admiration. They realized that Pat had shared with them his first, most honest reaction to the music. Pat agreed that he had done a pretty neat thing, but . . . *brave*? What was brave about it? When some of the other boys assured him that they could not have done it, Pat arrived at some new conceptions that, combined with his earlier convictions about the importance of courage, helped him to become strikingly honest in talking about his feelings.

Pat became an abandoned dancer, and as the weeks passed he learned to be intimate and considerate with his friends, including his teachers. He still occasionally became pugnacious, but he would soon catch himself at it; toughness was no longer his only way of behaving.

To us, it seemed that Pat's gradual shedding of physical inhibition —in which shadow play provided an important advance—made it possible for him to do his ballet dance in class. The understanding of his own courage that he gained from the dance and his classmates' discussion of it enabled him to find pleasure in the exploration of sensitive ways of relating to people. Thus the physical freeing exercises help prepare people for new kinds of relationships.

IT'S NICE, BUT WHAT IS IT?

Although physical freeing is a vital element of improvisational drama, it seems to be difficult for many people to understand. We can only say that physical freeing has occurred when a person starts to move more freely, to try bodily movements he has never tried before, to learn what his body can do, and to overcome inhibitions.

The best way to understand physical freeing is to perform the exercises and experience the feelings of aliveness, looseness, and freedom. Freeing the muscles and senses helps some people discover hard-to-describe capacities they never knew they had. Movement therapy is a widely accepted part of group psychiatric treatment.

We start our classes with physical freeing activities because we have found that physical freeing is the best way to prepare for self-expression and learning about oneself. Because we think these exercises also help improve verbal expression, our improvisational drama courses rely heavily on nonverbal communication at the beginning. Like basketball players who sometimes wear heavy gloves in practice, our students do without words for a while to make themselves better communicators with words.

Nonverbal communication is especially important for adults and college or high school students who have developed sophisticated defenses, rituals, and pastimes that are largely dependent on words. Their chances of exploring new ways of behavior are much better if they can get started nonverbally. Nonverbal does not mean only nontalking. Teachers sometimes have to warn students against playing charades or silent lip talking. These are simply inefficient forms of verbal communication, and their use defeats the effort to achieve physical directness.

The rest of this chapter is devoted to representative physical freeing activities.

1. *Isolated Body Movements, Standing, To Music.* This exercise provides a way of easing the group into movement. Before doing the exercise for the first time, the teacher might dance before the class, looking ludicrously awkward, and then say something like, "Nobody can look any sillier than I just did."

Then, moving to the music chosen for its lively, simple beat, the teacher calls out parts of the body to be moved: hands, arms, shoulders, heads, hips, legs. "All together. All together, now! You can't stand in one spot!" The emphasis is on expansiveness. "Make it big! Bigger!"

2. *Isolated Body Movements, Standing, Without Music.* The students express emotions or states of being—fear, joy, rage, love,

contentment, freedom—using parts of the body first in isolation and then all together.

3. *Relaxation.* Either seated or lying down, the students isolate and relax each part of the body. The instructions are to concentrate on each part and then to let it go. Starting with the extremities, either the feet or hands, they work inward to the back, stomach, chest, shoulders, neck, face, finally concentrating their attention on the point between the eyes.

As they become relaxed, the students might be told to concentrate on their heartbeats and try to slow them down, or to concentrate on the blood coursing through their arteries and veins.

4. *Shadow Play.* This improvisation illustrates some principles and practices that apply to many physical freeing activities, and is particularly valuable early in the course.

To make shadows, we use a slide projector to throw a strong light against a wall-size white backdrop. The student is instructed not to talk. Positioned in front of the screen, eyes fixed on his shadow, he concentrates on making his shadow "come alive." The other students also keep their eyes fixed on the shadow. For some students, the teacher plays music on a record player. For others, there are alternating periods of music and silence as the teacher discovers whether the student can move more freely and imaginatively with or without music. In helping the student cut loose, the teacher might try more than one kind of music.

During the early phases of the course, students are helped to feel at ease if the teacher demonstrates the exercises. He might dance, examine his profile, or experiment with the things his shadow can do. Then he extends a hand to a student, leads him on stage, and leaves him there. If the student immediately gets caught up in making his shadow move and watching it, no instructions from the teacher are needed. If instructions are needed, they should be in the form of encouragement rather than commands. The teacher might say, "Let it go, baby. Let it go!" He does not really command the student, but attempts to liberate him from his own unconscious command that tells him he cannot move freely. All of the teacher's instructions should suggest, "Let it go, and it will come by itself."

If the student looks lost, or in need of more explicit instructions, the teacher should keep his calls open-ended and stress making the shadow alive and expansive: "Make it live! Make it come alive! Bigger! Make it bigger! Watch that shadow. Keep your eyes on the shadow. Concentrate only on the shadow!" If the student is still overcome with inhibition, the teacher may join him. Together they can make shadows such as that of a four-armed man.

Later, one student might be placed on stage to join another. Then others can be added, making a group shadow. The teacher might pair a student who makes small, tight movements with one whose moves are large and sweeping so that both may learn from their nonverbal interaction.

Concentration on the shadow by both the participant and his audience enables many students to do things that would be too frightening for them if they focused entirely on what they were doing and were conscious of being watched.

5. *Animals.* This exercise introduces the students to the purposeful use of bodily movement. In being a cat, the actor tries to use movements both deliberate and fluid. As a giraffe, he might try to stretch his body, or as a rat to use quick, jerky movements. The actor must think very carefully about the movements of the animal he is assigned to be and then use his entire body in a new way, discovering more about its possibilities and limitations.

The teacher should allow several minutes on this improvisation— enough time for each student to explore the animal movements fully and to feel free about moving in unusual ways before spectators. Students can be given their animal assignments just before they perform, or at the end of a class so they can think about it as homework for the next day.

6. *Inanimate Objects.* The students are assigned singly, in pairs, or in larger groups, to be an inanimate object: a washing machine, a clock, a pair of scissors, a typewriter, an uncomfortable chair, a comfortable chair, a lamp, a folding card table, a bag of potato chips. This exercise can be done by one group while the rest of the class watches. We often put all of the students into groups of two or three and have them all improvise at once, with a time limit of about two minutes. Or the entire class can participate in one group improvisa- tion of an object such as scissors.

7. *Mirror Images.* Two people are placed on the stage. The teacher tells them one is looking into a mirror, but does not say which is the observer and which is the image. If a student has been frozen in class, he can be paired with someone who is livelier and warmer.

This can be done with one pair at a time, or all members of the group can be paired and all do the improvisation at once. The students should be given enough time to go beyond the first ideas that occur to them.

8. *Walking.* The students walk about the room, either in an orderly circle or at random. The teacher calls out an instruction: "Walk like a teacher," then continues with a series of walking assignments such as a student, a principal, a bear, a black person, a white person, a cop, a bully, a coward. Or, "You're in New York City for the first time in your life, and you're walking down Broadway."

9. *Free Dancing.* The teacher starts a record ("The Blue Danube Waltz" is good), and announces that the auditorium is packed, "and you're going to dance as you never have before." He dances freely for a moment, then takes the hand of a student and guides him onto the stage. One at a time, he brings the other students onstage until all, including the teacher, are dancing about at once. The dance should continue long enough for the dancers to extend themselves.

BREAKING THE BODY BUBBLE

We are conditioned to have bubbles of space around our bodies. The nature and extent of one's bubble seem to depend on environmental influences, such as the traditions of one's culture. For most people, the distance required between oneself and others varies according to who the other person is. An American man, for instance, is more likely to feel trespassed against if a man penetrates his bubble and presses his body against him, as in a crowded subway, than if a woman does the same thing.

As people in a group practice penetrating one another's bubbles and having their own penetrated, they experience a sense of liberation and, often, greater freedom in verbal and physical expression.

1. *The Face Feel.*

Richly supplied with nerves and striated muscles the face is capable of the most varied expression. Because of its endowment with distance receptors it is the region where the person meets the world, as it were, head-on. Not only is it the region where most impressions are received, but its exposure to the outer world makes it the station for signals of rejection, threat, or invitation to others. Perhaps for this reason it is the center to which we give our chief attention when we are observing others. It is likewise the principal focus of emotional expression, and the region where most people locate their sense of self-hood. Its intimate connection with feeding and with vocal communication are further reasons for its strategic position among the expressive agents of the body.[1]

The face feel is a very powerful experience for many people. We vary the instructions for this exercise but not the attitude toward it. We take it very seriously and encourage intense concentration. In introducing it, we don't say anything about "face feel," as that in itself might produce giggles. The teacher begins by pairing the students. If there are an odd number, the teacher can take one student as his own partner. The partners face each other sitting cross-legged on the floor as close together as they can get.

The instructions on one occasion were, "Pretend that you're blind. You don't know what the face of the person opposite you is like. Use your hands to discover what that face is like. And, very quietly, tell that person some things about his face. Tell that person how his face is different from yours, or how your faces are alike."

After giving them enough time to learn more about those faces than they originally wanted to know, the roles of each pair were switched; the opposite partners were now blind. Afterwards, George started the discussion by asking, "Did you find any differences between your faces?"

Often, a nonverbal approach is used, with no talking at all during the exercise and no discussion afterward. The partners explore one another's faces, while the teacher helps them focus by urging, "Explore that face," or, "Really get to know that face." The students then show each other differences and similarities in their faces without talking, by using their hands to "discuss" one another's facial features. The partners can either alternate or explore each other's faces simultaneously. The face feel can be done with or without blindfolds. For a group that is less afraid to touch, even closing the eyes might be unnecessary.

Many people do not realize how inhibited they are about touching faces. Frequently, they will wish to stop with brushing their fingertips against foreheads, and will especially avoid touching the partner's mouth. What the teacher can or cannot do about this reluctance depends on his assessment of the students' attitudes toward physical freedom.

With one group of blindfolded graduate students, George exploded, "That's a face, god damn it! How can you get to know it if you don't feel it? Don't just touch it, *feel* it! How about the mouth?

Can you know a face if you don't know the mouth?" That approach worked very well with this group of young people who were aware of their tightness and eager to overcome it; they accepted George's assertive coaching and the exercise became a stirring experience for all of them.

Another group of twenty public school teachers were there because they had been ordered to be there and the school system was paying them for it. Under such conditions, the teacher must modify his expectations. Soothingly, George said, "How about that mouth? See how much you can learn about that mouth." Some appeared not to learn very much, but more assertive leadership probably would have hurt more than it helped.

2. *Mud Throw*. The students are told that they are standing in mud. The teacher might scoop up some mud and laughingly throw it on someone, saying, "Let's cover each other with mud!" This is always fun, and it is an odd kind of transition to physical contact. There is almost no real contact, but the imaginary person-to-person sloshing of mud has some of the same liberating effect.

3. *Point of Contact*. The students are paired off. As the teacher starts the music he tells them, "Touch each other with one part of your bodies. Just one part. And move to the music. When I call change, touch each other with a *different* part of your bodies." After a dozen changes or more, with no repetition allowed, students make some imaginative contacts.

4. *The Sardine Can*. The teacher instructs the students to lie on their backs, side by side, on the floor. They are to keep their backs on the floor and squeeze together toward the middle, as the teacher cheers them on. Then they spread out and repeat the exercise several times.

5. *Telephone Booth*. The teacher indicates a circle about four feet in diameter on the floor, using the spotlight if it is strong enough, or marking it with chalk or a loop of string.

"This is a telephone booth. You are wild college freshmen. Get into this telephone booth. Every one of you must be inside it in two minutes!"

6. *Group Sway*. The people walk together into a round huddle— tight, but not uncomfortably packed as in the telephone booth exercise. They sway to the music, which the teacher changes periodically.

PHYSICAL EXPRESSION: THE ROCK

People tell a great deal about themselves through their bodily movements. As the teacher gains insight, he picks up cues from his students that may be useful in helping the students later. Shadow play, for instance, tells the teacher which students will have trouble expressing themselves, which are able to use their imaginations freely, which are facile emulators, and which are simply scared stiff of people.

In warm-ups one day, a class of adults gave some interesting cues while doing The Rock, a physical exercise calling for strong concentration and belief in what one is doing.

The instructions were, "Look at the floor in front of you. There's a rock. It's a big rock. Bend over and feel it. You're going to have to lift it over your head, and it's going to be heavy. You know just how big it is. Now pick that rock up. Pick it up. You've got to pick it up!"

The warm-ups leader, a public school teacher, urged them on until all of them, straining and panting, had their rocks above their heads. Then he called, "Ho-o-old it. . . . Drop it!"

On the way up, a very feminine young woman dropped her rock several times.

A talented, competent young man, who placed a high value on orderly processes, felt his rock carefully. Using his muscles and skeletal structure in the safest, most efficient way, he lifted the rock smoothly and with just the right amount of strain.

Another man in the class was extraordinarily unaware of his selfishness and lack of consideration for people. He swung his imaginary rock off the floor with such gusto that he would have knocked down the people on either side of him had his rock been real. Staggering about the room, grunting loudly, he bumped several colleagues without seeming to notice. When the order came to "drop it," he slammed his rock onto the head of a woman in front of him.

An administrator somehow managed to pick up his rock in such a way that it was cradled in his arms like a baby. With a blank and helpless expression, he staggered around the room with his rock cuddled against his chest. The administrator's ineptitude in lifting the rock was characteristic of his tendency to start something before thinking about how it should be done, thus creating problems to which he clung, seeming to feel that undoing the problems or starting over would be an unbearable admission of failure. When he realized that the other people already had their rocks high in the air, he shifted and raised his rock with an unrealistic move that would have resulted in smashed toes had the burden been real.

We do not suggest that teachers should pass on observations such as these. Most people are infuriated at the thought of anyone "figuring them out" by watching their movements. These examples serve only to illustrate the kind of consistent expression that occurs in simple physical activities, and to remind us of something too easily underestimated or forgotten: the importance of the physical in the makeup of each of us.

NOTES

1. Gordon W. Allport, *Personality* (New York: Holt & Co., 1937), p. 481.

Seven:
CONCENTRATION

In Western culture, writes Erich Fromm,

> When we do one thing, we are already thinking of the next thing, of the moment when we can stop what we are doing now. . . . *If one is truly concentrated, the very thing one is doing at this moment is the most important thing in life.* If I talk to someone, if I read something, if I walk—whatever it is, if I do it in a concentrated fashion, there is nothing more important than what I am doing in the here and now . . . there is no past or future as a real experience. There is only the here and now. Quite obviously, there can be no true awareness and no true response except *in the here and now, that is to say, in the attitude of full commitment to whatever I do, see, feel at this very moment.*[1] (Emphasis added.)

Concentration is best learned through pleasurable disciplines. In Zen archery, for example, the archer concentrates so fully that target, archer, bow, and arrow all become one. By mastering his discipline in this way, the student also comes into harmony with the philosophical attitude of Zen.[2]

Concentration in improvisational drama is learned largely through acting. In order for the actor to give a concrete characterization—to become specific about who he is and what his tasks are—he must learn to concentrate. In the usual progression of an improvisational drama course, attention is given to developing concentration from the first physical freeing exercises. When the group moves out of the physical freeing phase, concentration is emphasized even more strongly, and strengthening concentration remains a vital purpose of the warm-ups in every phase of development.

Because concentration is needed in every discipline, teachers have found these exercises and techniques useful in all kinds of school situations. By concentrating on seemingly unimportant situations, many students are able to raise their level of consciousness. This kind of phenomenological training helps clear away the irrelevant exterior clutter and inner tensions that frequently block and distort perception. A person who is able to clear a path for perceptions—an ability some psychologists call percipience—often feels that perceptions seem to leap out at him.

The concentration phase of an improvisational drama course trains people to think specifically. Concentration on externals—listening and watching—is necessary if the student is to learn from his or another person's experience or other people's reflections of his experience.

The involvement attained through physical freeing, concentration, and believability paves the way for a high level of learning and creativity. Rollo May describes the creative act as "an encounter" that may or may not involve "voluntaristic effort," or "will power." May writes,

A healthy child's play, for example, also has the essential features of encounter, and we know it is one of the important prototypes of adult creativity. The essential point is not the presence or absence of voluntaristic effort, but the degree of absorption, the degree of intensity; there must be a specific quality of *engagement*. [3]

Many artists affirm that concentration is essential to creativity. As Saul Bellow has said, "I feel that art has something to do with the achievement of stillness in the midst of chaos. A stillness which characterizes prayer, too, and the eye of the storm. I think that art has something to do with an arrest of attention in the midst of distraction." [4] Our concentration exercises help students arrest their attention in the midst of all that distraction.

FROM EXTERNAL TO INTERNAL

The initial concentration exercises are simple tasks used by acting coaches for decades, such as counting things without being distracted by the surroundings. The students can be paired off and instructed to count one another's eyelashes (a favorite of Stanislavski), for example, or the dots or squares in the ceiling, or the lines in the floor or the palms of their hands, or the orange blocks on the teacher's shirt.

With these simple tasks, the students begin to concentrate. The next step is to transfer that concentration inside themselves. One way of doing this is to switch from counting visible external objects to counting from memory. The students sit in meditation posture and silently count all the smooth, blue, round, dangerous, cold, sweet, or bitter things they know. Since there is no external object to concentrate on, the mind is more likely to drift or lose focus. Throughout the exercise, the teacher encourages the students to be specific and hold their focus.

More demanding internal concentration can be stimulated by such exercises as tracing the events of a day. The students start by sitting quietly with their eyes closed. After they are relaxed, the teacher instructs them to think of a day—that day, another recent one, or a day they enjoyed so much they would like to live it over again.

"You are going to trace the events of that day," the teacher says. "Mentally relive exactly what you did. Begin with waking up. Was it chilly or warm? What colors were in the room? Concentrate on the sounds, the smells, the feelings you had."

The students have six or seven minutes to concentrate on this task. Although this exercise is more internal than the two previous exercises, it is still primarily objective since the students are concentrating on what they actually did or observed. Later in the class, after doing a more active exercise, the students are instructed to go back to the beginning of the day they concentrated on before. This time, they are to concentrate on and recapture the feelings they had during that day. This exercise takes their concentration still deeper and helps them to start being conscious of their feelings in a way that may lead to better self-understanding.

The process of focusing concentration in character improvization is similar. Suppose the student is to portray a father who is taking his son for a conference with a teacher. He should be specific about this father. How does he stand? What is his facial expression? How does he move? He must concentrate on how his character thinks and feels, so that he will respond appropriately to the unfolding situation. He might get into his role by concentrating on his own father, another specific father, or a composite.

ENCOURAGING CONCENTRATION

We introduced our sixth- to eighth-grade boys to the concept of concentration on the second day of class. Walking about the stage, George said, "When I'm up here, everybody is watching me. So what am I going to do?"

"Run!" one boy said, jumping up and running from the room. "He says 'run,'" George mused. (He said nothing about the departure of the boy, who later rejoined the class unobtrusively.) Some other suggestions were offered, and the boys decided that the important thing was to not think about the audience. George suggested that while on stage each student could build an imaginary wall around himself. The boys scattered around the stage and actually built imaginary walls with their hands.

We advise students to wring their hands or clench and unclench them as they build up creative tension and concentration for their performances. George, taking quick nervous strides around the stage, making eye contact with each boy in turn, might say intensely: "Start wringing your hands. Let's go! C'mon, tension, tension! Vitality! You gotta be alive. Concentrate!" Sometimes he takes the actors to a back corner of the stage, where they may stay and concentrate until they are ready to act. "Tense your hands, and think about what you are going to do," he might say. "There's nobody here but you."

From time to time, before the class does improvisations, the teacher might remind them of their walls. "Erect an imaginary wall around yourself. A wall between you and the audience. Because if you don't, what you do won't be real. And it must be real to have value."

Younger students sometimes need coaching on their concentration as members of the audience. This is best done as an assignment, rather than as a prohibition. The teacher might say, "You need to concentrate to be a good actor. But you also need to concentrate to be a good member of the audience. And when you're quietly concentrating, that helps the actors concentrate, too."

If the students are restless during an improvisation, the teacher should do a brief concentration exercise. He might say, "Look at me. Look carefully. Concentrate. Look at my face as if you'd never seen it before. Look hard at me. See it like you'd never seen it before."

SAMPLE CONCENTRATION EXERCISES

Ballpassing

A natural for children, this activity has proved popular with people of all ages. The teacher supplies a number of rubber balls, about the size of baseballs, in a hat or other container. The students and teacher sit on the floor in a close circle. The teacher takes one ball and hands it to the student on his right, saying, "Keep it going." Each student should receive the ball in his left hand, switch it to his right, and put it in the left hand of the person to his right. When the ball gets about halfway around, the teacher starts another in the same direction. As the students catch on, the teacher keeps adding balls until there are almost as many balls making the rounds as there are people.

The speed can be varied, and the direction can be reversed. Or the balls can be bounced, with the receivers catching them on first bounce.

In another variation, the participants close their eyes and roll two balls around the circle. The teacher instructs, "Use your sixth sense to know where the balls are without peeking."

Concentrating On a Person

Students are paired and told, "Look carefully at the person opposite you. Concentrate totally on what you see of that person until I tell you to stop." Many people have not really looked carefully and long at another person since childhood; two or three minutes is long enough for the students to explore each other's features visually in great detail.

Next, the teacher says, "Concentrate on the thoughts and feelings of the student you have been looking at. How does he feel? How does he think? What is that person *really* like?"

In concentrating on this task, and talking about it afterward, students learn how they experience other people, and how they combine reality, projection, and wishful thinking in their concepts of others. The discussion is also valuable to a person who has been observed, because he experiences other people's experience of him.

In a variation on this exercise, the students sit in a relaxed position with their eyes closed, and the teacher tells them a common noun representing a person on which they are to concentrate. "The word is *friend* (or father, mother, cop, teacher, soldier, athlete, president). Think of a specific friend." The students must think specifically about the physical qualities of that person—how he looks, stands, sounds, and moves. The next instruction is, "Concentrate on your feelings about that person. What are all your positive feelings toward him? List your positive feelings. What are all your negative feelings?" In the ensuing discussion, the students may be very clear and objective about how they feel and why. Or they may not, which is almost as revealing.

Concentrating on a Feeling

A student is put on the stage and told to portray the word *fear*. Or the word might be *joy, love, disgust,* or any other feeling.

Discussion of this exercise is sometimes quite helpful in clarifying the students' ideas about concentration. When Doug was asked to portray fear, he showed annoyance, anger, frustration, disgust—but no fear. In the discussion, several of the boys were quick to point out Doug's deviation from his assignment. They asked Doug what had been in his mind while he tried to act out fear. Not much of anything, he admitted. He had not been able to think of something specific that he feared, and therefore had been unable to concentrate on fear. In that discussion, nobody was probing to find out why Doug was unable to concentrate on fear. The discussion was concerned with what mental technique Doug had used in failing to concentrate on his task, and what technique he might have used to succeed. We do not push the discussion past this point; if the students carry it farther, we do not stop them.

TROUBLESHOOTING

By close observation, the teacher learns to recognize when the students' concentration is drifting. A glance at the audience, stereotypical or inappropriate action or dialogue are signs of lack of concentration. Our inner-city boys sometimes betrayed their loss of concentration by getting rough. In such a case, the teacher might stop the improvisation with *freeze,* and then say something like, "Get your concentration. Get it back. Are you ready? Go." Or he might say, "Remember your task. Think about your task. Concentrate on it. Go."

If several people in the group are goofing off, it is usually effective to discuss the situation with the class in terms of concentration.

CHANGING THROUGH CONCENTRATION

At the beginning of the course, Joey had the attention span of a small child. He got his share of attention by being the silliest kid in the class. George assigned Joey some very childish roles, and he threw himself into them. After class one day, Joey said that he was going to concentrate on not doing anything goofy for a whole day to see if people would stop treating him as if he were goofy. Each day he decided to concentrate for one more day on not doing the silly things that had become habitual with him. He also said he was practicing concentration exercises at home. He was the only student we can recall ever making such a claim.

His classmates began to treat him with respect. Some of them told him in class that they were glad he had stopped acting dumb. One day Joey's mother came to school to find out what was happening in his improvisational drama class. At home, she said, Joey had become "a different person," more mature and reasonable.

Joey's understanding of his behavior came from his own discoveries, with the aid of the mirror provided by his classmates and other people in his life. Having discovered his shortcomings himself, he was able to deal with them without feeling blamed. In looking for a way to change what he did not like about himself, he was attracted to the aspect of improvisational drama that he needed most, the concentration exercises.

NOTES

1. Erich Fromm, "The Creative Attitude," in *Creativity and Its Cultivation,* ed. Harold H. Anderson (New York: Harper and Row, 1959), p. 49.

2. Eugen Herrigel, *Zen in the Art of Archery* (New York: Pantheon, 1953).

3. Rollo May, "Nature of Creativity," in *Creativity and Its Cultivation,* pp. 58-59.

4. Interview by Gordon Lloyd Harper in *Writers at Work,* Paris Review Interviews, 3d Series, ed. George Plimpton (New York: Viking, 1967), p. 190.

Eight:
BELIEVABILITY

By this time, the boys were aiming for believability in their improvisations. They had practiced simple exercises to develop believability, and George often started the discussions following improvisations by asking, "Was it believable?"

The boys knew that believability in improvisation depends on getting into character well enough to react spontaneously to the other actor. With only a minute or two in which to think, they had to call on models that they knew well for the concrete details needed to create the physical actions of their characters. Thus, although nothing is said about improvising characters "that are relevant to your lives," the emphasis on believability, combined with the spontaneity called for by improvisation, encourages characterizations that have important meaning for the actors.

One day George called Ray and Robby on stage. "You are a father," he told Ray. Then he turned to Robby and said, "You are his son."

Although he was not usually a dominant person, Ray, who came from a family with eleven children, assumed his role immediately. He became a cruel drunkard whose only desire was to torment anyone close to him. He reeled drunkenly about the stage shouting harshly at his son. Robby, playing the son, begged Ray not to hit him. As Ray drew back his arm, Robby fell abjectly to the floor, covering his head with his arms. He was totally submissive, never talking back as Ray cursed and threatened him.

After a few minutes, George froze the improvisation and seated Ray and Robby in the center for a discussion. "I believed it!" Frank and Doug exclaimed simultaneously. Everyone agreed that Ray and Robby had believed what they were doing, and so had the audience.

"Ray, he really seem drunk and mean," Chet volunteered.

"My father acts that way sometimes—you know, like when he's drunk," Frank said.

Finally, Doug asked Ray if he had believed it. "Yes," Ray said softly. "What I did was to play my own father." He explained that his father was "always drunk and always beating the kids and stuff."

When the conversation turned to Robby, all the boys, including Ray, said they believed him. They all agreed that in such a situation they would behave much as Robby had. In fact, it was evident that some of them had been in similar situations.

Then George asked the boys to play the scene again. "But this time, Robby, you must play your role a different way. You must show us an alternative." This time, Robby stood on his feet and told the bullying father, "Why don't you go to bed and sleep it off?" When Ray grabbed for him, Robby twisted away and ran, calling back, "If you chase me, I'm gonna call the cops!"

Because the boys had believed what they were doing, they were able to explore alternatives and consider the possibility of exerting more control over their destinies in some ways. This process was possible because they had started by being specific and believable in their task—by honestly portraying what they had seen, heard, thought, and felt. They had not talked at length or in depth about their fathers, but they had shared a believable experience.

The emphasis on specificity begins in the concentration phase, and work on believability grows naturally out of concentration. To be believable, one must concentrate on the physical actions of the character he is portraying. If he is portraying a thought or feeling, rather than a person, he needs to come up with physical actions to convey it. To give a believable portrayal of an abstraction is difficult, so we give this assignment only after the students have succeeded at more concrete exercises.

In one of our believability exercises, a student is put on the stage and told to react to a word. The word is an abstract emotion such as love, anger, or fear. The student is expected to represent the word physically. The first students who do this are usually quite confident; being an abstraction is not as threatening to them as acting out a concrete situation. But many of them discover that believability is impossible in a purely abstract role. To believe what they are doing and to be believed, they must become specific.

In one of our classes, Jack, a student at Antioch College, was instructed to be angry. He raged around shouting curses, beating his fists against the wall, grimacing, and generally acting out anger as an abstraction. In the discussion his classmates said he was not exactly unbelievable, but they did not believe him. He really had not communicated the feeling of anger. Jack tried it again, portraying a conversation with his father about why he wanted to drop out of school. His father did not understand; then Jack did not understand his father. Jack built up the anger in himself at the same time that he developed an empathetic, emotional understanding of the situation in his audience.

Believability is not confined to realistic acting. A portrayal may be a grotesque caricature of reality and still be believable if the player believes it. He may use exaggerations similar to those in dreams or in the crayon drawings of a child, but if the performance is an emotionally true depiction of the player's feelings, the sensitive spectator will be convinced.

BELIEVABILITY WARM-UP ACTIVITIES

In dreaming up believability warm-up exercises, the teacher should give free rein to his imagination. We start with the concrete and simple, then gradually become more complex in our assignments.

1. *The Balloon.* Young children particularly enjoy this exercise, in which the teacher tells the students they are empty balloons. Then they are pumped full of air. When they have gotten as big as they can get, the teacher tells them to get still bigger. Then they start to deflate. When all the air is out of them, the teacher tells them to inflate again. "Bigger. Get bigger in the arms. Bigger in the chest. Bigger in the head. Bigger in the hands." When they are over-inflated again, the teacher might dart about the room puncturing each balloon so that they pop in rapid succession.

This kind of exercise challenges the student's imagination. For instance, when the teacher suddenly "pops" him, the student must make an instant decision as to how one pops. He might collapse to the floor, spin crazily around the room, or leap in the air and yell "pop."

2. *Melting and Evaporating.* The teacher instructs the students, "You are a statue made of ice. You are all ice. Think about it. Believe it. You are starting to feel the warm rays of the sun. You begin to melt."

After the students have melted into pools of water on the floor, they begin to evaporate. They become lacy, fluffy clouds floating in the air. If the instructions are given in a soothing voice and the students believe what they are doing, this can be quite a refreshing exercise, with infinite variations. For example, the students could be seeds, springing out of the ground and growing into tall, spreading trees.

3. *Reacting to an Object.* An object such as a toy pistol, a wastebasket, a sheet, or an old hat is put on the stage, and the actor is instructed to do something with it. If the same object is used by another actor, the teacher tells him to do something different with it.

4. *Reacting to Pictures.* A slide is projected on the wall, and the teacher says, "Concentrate on it. Believe it is real. I'm going to bring you up here one at a time, and you're going to react to the picture in some way."

5. *Tug-Of-War.* A tug-of-war is set up with half the students on each end of a heavy rope. The teacher should try to stimulate competitiveness. As the competition becomes frenzied and one side is winning, the teacher calls *freeze* and instructs the students to think about what they just did, how they did it, and how they felt while doing it. "Do a replay in your head of everything you did and felt in the tug-of-war. Now, try to do just what you did before. Try to recapture the same actions and feelings. Ready. Begin!"

After taking a few minutes to think about it, the students repeat the action using an imaginary rope. After an element essential to the reality of the situation is removed, the actors are still able to make the situation believable by continuing to concentrate on the same physical actions. In this way, the exercise demonstrates the essence of believability.

6. *Telephone Conversation.* The actor sits center stage with a telephone. His assignment might be, "Call someone you know," or "You're very angry with someone, and you're talking with that person on the phone," or "Call someone and ask for help with something that bothers you."

In this exercise the actor must make two roles believable—his own and that of the person on the other end of the line. At least he must pause long enough to allow the imaginary person to respond naturally.

7. *The Wall.* The instruction is, "Go to the wall. Become one with it." Although the effect of this exercise is internal and there is not

much to see, the teacher should allow plenty of time for the students to experience it.

8. *Claustrophobia.* "The Walls are closing in and you have to push them apart." With the anxiety building in his voice, the teacher keeps reminding the students that, despite all of their straining, the boxes they are in continue to get smaller. He might also free some of the students and suggest that they try to help the others.

BELIEVABILITY THROUGH SPECIFICITY

To become believable, the student must be able to use his body, knowledge, and experience, including emotional experience, and to make instantaneous and specific decisions about who he is and how he responds and relates to other characters.

Suppose one actor is to play a student and another a teacher in an after-school confrontation over the student's alleged misbehavior. The actor who is playing the teacher must go through certain steps in creating his role. First, he considers the personality of the teacher he is to portray, recalling specific teachers he has seen in action. Then he must imagine the personal appearance of his character. How will he move and act? How will he talk? What kinds of things will he say?

Next, the "teacher" must decide what preceded the action—why he is reprimanding the boy. In this skit, as in others based on realistic situations, the students are allowed to confer before starting the exercise. Was the boy fighting with another student? Was he cheating on a test? With little time for invention, students will frequently portray situations they have experienced or witnessed. The choices the improvisational actor makes in becoming specific often lead him into portrayals that illuminate his experience.

Nine:
RELATIONSHIPS

Relationships are the lifeblood of improvisational drama. The other elements—physical freeing, concentration, believability—all contribute to the exploration of relationships between people.

In one of the plainest improvisations for exploring relationships, the teacher guides two students onto the stage and tells them, "Do whatever you'd like." Or he might simply make an expansive gesture with his hands to indicate, "It's all yours." To minimize the students' reliance on verbal rituals, they are often told not to talk during this exercise.

One of the first times we used this improvisation, the instruction was, "Form a relationship—without talking." This assignment turned out to be misleading, as the sixth- and seventh-grade boys in the class interpreted "relationship" to mean "friendship." But the activity was successful anyway, as the boys made some important discoveries about their ways of relating to other people.

George put Larry, a slender, black twelve-year-old, and Lorraine, a black secretary at the Advancement School, on the stage and told them to form a relationship without talking.

Lorraine put her hand on Larry's shoulder and smiled warmly. Larry jerked petulantly away and strutted to the other side of the stage, where he stood staring into the darkness, arms folded tightly, his back to Lorraine. She followed him and continued to appeal sweetly, trying to establish a friendly relationship, but Larry repeatedly turned away to keep his back toward her.

After a few minutes, George stopped the improvisation. The two actors sat center stage for the discussion. "Did they accomplish their task?" George asked. "Did they form a relationship?" The boys said Lorraine did try to establish a relationship, but Larry did not. Obviously, they equated "relationship" with "friendship."

George whispered something to Lorraine, then put the two of them back on the stage and gave them the same task. This time, when Larry turned his back to Lorraine she walked to the opposite side of the stage, turned her back to Larry, and stared off stage. Eventually he sneaked a look over his shoulder and saw that she was not noticing him. He sidled up to her, got in a position where she could hardly help seeing him, then turned his back to her and ostentatiously "ignored" her once again. Lorraine continued to ignore Larry, just as George had secretly instructed her. In the discussion that followed, the boys were quick to figure out that Larry's rejection of Lorraine was a way of developing a relationship with her, and that choosing to ignore her was a purposeful action.

The boys remarked, "He was trying to make her feel bad," and, "He was controlling her." "Hey! Larry did the same thing this morning with one of his teachers," a boy noted. Another said, "He does it to me sometimes." "I do it to my parents all the time," Larry reflected. "And it works, too."

Another boy said he often used this tactic very effectively with teachers. He had found that if he put a bit of "you don't care about me" into the rejection, teachers went out of their way to help him and often excused him from unpleasant tasks. The discussion continued fruitfully as the boys documented the ways they manipulated parents and teachers, bringing out fine points about what techniques worked best with which teachers.

In discussing improvisations the important questions are, "How did they relate to one another?" and, "What did they do?" It may be productive for the students to discuss whether the relationship was good or bad, but usually the teacher should neither initiate nor take part in such discussions.

The improvisation discussed above was not planned to help Larry recognize the way he manipulated people or to prove any other point. Larry determined the content when he chose to develop his relationship with Lorraine by rejecting her. George's instructions to Lorraine helped the students clarify their thinking, and the boys pursued the idea in their discussion. For Larry, it was a breakthrough. He continued to gain in understanding, and near the end of the term his mother enthusiastically reported that he seldom pouted any more.

For us too the improvisation between Larry and Lorraine and the subsequent discussion had concrete results. Since then we have not told people to have relationships. Kids usually do not understand what "relationship" means; and also, the instruction is redundant. People in a room together always do have some sort of relationship.

INTRODUCING RELATIONSHIPS CONCRETELY: EXERCISES

When the group is ready to focus on relationships, we try to keep the initial explorations concrete by starting with exercises that use a physical prop and in which there is no talking. Later, exercises with no props are used, and finally we move on to improvisations in which people talk.

1. *The Rope.* Two people are brought on stage and told they may not talk. Each is given an end of a rope about six feet long and the instruction, "You must keep this rope taut at all times."

An alternative is to place a stick about two feet long between the midriffs of the two participants and instruct them to dance to recorded music. After the improvisation the teacher may start the discussion by asking, "What happened?"

In our classes, we have found that the answers become more perceptive as the exercise is repeated with different people. "Doug didn't let Frank do nothin' he wanted to. Everytime Frank move the rope one way, Doug, he move back the other way. He didn't give any at all." "He led Charles around like he was on a leash. Like he was a dog!" "Each one kept waitin' for the other one to do somethin'."

When Mike found that he could roll himself up in the rope to put a friendly arm around Wilt, a classmate appreciated his initiative: "He kept the rope tight, just like you said, and still got close to Wilt and be buddies."

But discovering these answers is not as important as discovering questions. Implicitly, the students seek answers to such unphrased questions as, Did they share, or did one lead and the other follow? Were they equals, or was one dominant and the other submissive? Were they concerned about one another's wishes, or did each try to force his own thing? Did they make their wishes known to each other?

In discussing what has happened in these exercises, the teacher need only interject an occasional, "Why?" As the students become involved in such unstated problems as, "Why do some people force their wills, and why do others allow themselves to be led?" they often discover that the answers are implicit in the questions.

2. *Relating through Rhythm.* Two, three, or four students are seated on the stage in front of drums and told they may not speak. Or they may be put on an empty stage and told, "The only sound you may make is clapping." The last instruction is, "Begin when you feel you want to."

The discussion of this exercise is often concerned with the same topics brought out by the rope or stick exercises. Did the participants work together harmoniously? Did one person dominate? Did each of them do his own thing? Did they express anything? Did they show concern for one another? How did they relate?

3. *Relating without Words.* In this exercise, two or three students are placed on the stage and given a task such as, "You may do anything you like except talk."

In one class, George placed Howard and Joey in diagonally opposite corners of the stage facing one another, with Al in the middle facing Howard. When told to begin, they stood silently for a moment. Suddenly Howard threw an imaginary ball to Joey, who caught it and threw it back. As they threw the ball back and forth, Al kept trying to intercept. After a few unsuccessful tries, he leapt and caught Howard's throw. With perfect communcation, he and Howard immediately changed places, and the game continued with Howard in the middle. It was such a remarkably realistic game of monkey-in-the-middle that it reminded us of the tennis scene in the film *Blowup.*

Afterwards, the three boys were thrilled. "We were just so *real!*" Howard bubbled. They had experienced each other in the context of the game, and no one had faltered in awareness. The boys had discovered that acting forces us to concentrate on how we relate to others. One cannot develop a situation or complete a task involving another person without being aware of what the other is doing and how he reacts.

4. *Secret Tasks.* In this exercise each actor is given his assignment separately, so that no one knows what any of the others is supposed to be. For example, one actor might be told, "You are the father of a teen-age girl. A young man is coming to take your daughter out on a date." The other actor might be told, "You are a washing machine repairman. You are going to this house to repair a washing machine. You are to accomplish your task without telling what your occupation is and without mentioning 'washing machine.' "

If these improvisations go badly, it is usually because the situation was too complicated. The best situations start with simple instructions to two actors. After the improvisation starts, one or two more may be given secret tasks and make their entrances as the skit is in progress.

5. *Parties.* Every term we assigned our middle-school students to act out a party in which they played themselves. The kids really were just having a party in a room, but because they had been assigned to act they seemed to rise above themselves socially. They were more charming and considerate than usual, and nobody rushed to wolf down the food—at least not until after class.

In a typical party class, the students entered to find a table against one wall laden with goodies. After the students were seated George said, "Robby and Carole are going to give a party. I was invited, but I have already called to say that I might not be able to make it. If I do come, I will be late."

Robby and Carole greeted the "guests" as they came in, and the party was off to a great start. When it started to drag, there was a knock at the door, and George made his grand entrance to the welcoming cheers of the class.

One of the highlights of the party was the impersonation game. Each student impersonated someone else in the group, and the others guessed who it was. The spirit was so high that the boys took the caricatures of themselves in good fun, with no evidence of hurt feelings. One of the funniest impersonators strutted about bellowing "freeze."

6. *Other Activities Emphasizing Relationships.* There are any number of variations on activities in which people tell something about themselves or how they feel about someone else. In warm-ups, people may be put in groups of two or three and told, "Tell the other person something he doesn't know about you," or, "Tell him something you like or don't like about him or yourself," or, "Tell him what you think he was like at the age of seven," or, "Tell him something you'd like to change about yourself, or about him." Thirty to sixty seconds should be allotted for each of these simple tasks.

Assignments for improvisations might include: Do something you do only when you are alone; return to the age that you would go back to if you could; if you could change something about yourself that you don't like, how would you change it, or show something you like, or are afraid of, and so on. Improvisations challenge the teacher's imagination too. And of course the teacher must be alert to cues from students on which to base improvisations.

EXPERIENCING OTHER PEOPLE

In *The Politics of Experience,* R. D. Laing writes about the ways in which people experience one another.

> I cannot avoid trying to understand your experience, because although I do not experience your experience, which is invisible to me (and nontastable, nontouchable, nonsmellable, and inaudible), yet I experience you *as experiencing.*
>
> I do not experience your experience. But I experience you as experiencing. I experience myself as experienced by you. And I experience you as experiencing yourself as experienced by me. And so on.
>
> The study of the experience of others is based on inferences I make, from my experience of you experiencing me, about how you are experiencing me experiencing you experiencing me . . . .
>
> Social phenomenology is the science of my own and of others' *experience.* It is concerned with the relation between my experience of you and your experience of me. That is, with *interexperience.* It is concerned with your behavior and my behavior *as I experience it,* and your and my behavior *as you experience it.*[1]

From the point of view of the social phenomenologist, improvisational drama students learn from interexperience. In moments of intense awareness, insights about the experiences of the group seem to leap out at the members of the group. Our inquiry into relationships is concrete, and we hope that improvisational drama will help the students gain experience in seeing other people as people rather than as objects bearing labels for such superficial abstractions as skin color, popularity, unpopularity, social class, clothes, usefulness, or nonusefulness.

Erich Fromm describes some of the difficulties we all face in trying to experience people concretely: "What we experience when we see people is not customarily different from what we experience when we see things." When we believe we see a person, Fromm continues, we actually see marginal things such as education and social class.

> We see in the concrete person an abstraction, just as he sees an abstraction in himself and in us. We do not want to see more. We share the general phobia of being too close to a person, of penetrating through the surface to his core, and so we prefer to see little, no more than is necessary for our particular dealings with the other person. This kind of marginal knowledge corresponds to an inner state of indifference in our feeling toward the other person . . .

Projections, greed, folly, and anger make us see people unrealistically, as well as marginally and superficially, Fromm writes, and the goal of experiencing people concretely is

To see the other person . . . objectively, that is, without projections and without distortions, and this means overcoming in oneself those neurotic "vices" which necessarily lead to projections and distortions. It means to wake up fully to the awareness of reality, inside and outside of oneself. To put it in other words: only if one has reached a degree of inner maturity which reduces projection and distortion to a minimum can one experience creatively. . . .

To see a person or a thing in this sense of utmost reality is the condition for giving a realistic response. Most responses are as unreal and purely mental as most awareness. . . . if I see a person suffering in front of me . . . I react with my heart, with my hands and my legs. I suffer with him. I have the impulse to help, and I carry out the impulse. Even when confronted with the concreteness of another person's suffering or another person's happiness, however, many people react only marginally. They "think" the proper feeling, they do the proper action, and yet they remain distant. To respond in a realistic sense means that I respond with my real human power, that of suffering, of joy, of understanding, to the reality of the "object" which experiences something. I respond to the person as he is; to the experience of the other person as it is. I respond not only with my brain or my eyes or my ears. I respond as the whole person I am. I think with my belly. I see with my heart. When I respond to an object with the real powers in me, which are fitted to respond to it, the object ceases to be an object. I become one with it. I cease to be the observer. I cease to be the judge. This kind of response occurs in a situation of complete relatedness, in which seer and seen, observer and observed, become one, although at the same time they remain two.[2]

It is possible for both participants and observers to gain insight into themselves and others through improvisations without talking about what has happened, but discussions are often valuable because they allow the students to share insights and learn how others react to the same experience. The discussions also help them develop honesty and the ability to accept and give criticism.

"FAT ALBERT" AND THE CAGE

Sometimes just the act of discussing oneself with unusual honesty helps to clear away some of the stumbling blocks in one's relationships. Such an incident began when George, in the spotlight, cried, "I'm in a glass cage! I can't talk to you, but you can talk to me. Communicate with me!"

The sixth- and seventh-grade students circled him shouting insults. "Look at that thing in the cage!" "Ha, haaa! He can't get out!" Howard shouted the most obnoxious insults. Called Fat Albert by the other boys, Howard had the heft and waddle of Bill Cosby's comic character. A black boy from the slums, he was likely to react to any difficult situation with, "I'll beat the shit out of you!" The boys consistently rejected his desperate attempts to assume leadership.

As the taunting students circled George in his imaginary cage, one boy exclaimed, "Let's help him get out!" The tone of the improvisation changed immediately. "We want to help you!" shouted the boys, and "Let's break the glass and get him out." Suddenly George relaxed and smiled; the "cage" dissolved. George sat cross-legged on the floor and the boys gathered around him. "What was it about?" he asked them. "What were you doing?" The boys talked excitedly, trying to explain their actions. Then George asked, "What *was* that glass cage?" "It doesn't have to be a glass cage," one boy said intensely.

"What do you mean?"

"Well, you know, George, like, lots of times when I'm with my friends, I feel like I'm in a glass cage."

Then Howard's gravelly voice said, "Whenever I'm at a party, I feel like I'm in a cage." He was more serious and revealed more of himself than he ever had before in class. From that day he started changing, gaining confidence in himself and winning the respect of the other boys. By the time he had finished his fourteen weeks at the Advancement School and was ready to return to public school, Howard had become the acknowledged leader of that class.

The cage exercise is useful, but the teacher should be extremely cautious about putting a student inside the cage. If the members of the class have much hidden hostility, as many urban kids do, they are likely to unleash it on the person in the cage. If the student is at all lacking in confidence he could be hurt or frightened, whether he showed it or not. If a student is put into the cage, those circling him should be prohibited from talking at first. Protruding tongues and extended middle fingers are easier to handle than verbal insults. When there is substantial hostility in the group, only the teacher should be put in the cage.

THE GROUP FEELING

One of the most constructive developments in improvisational drama classes is the growth of the kind of group feeling of which Eric Berne writes, "in spite of the now established value of group therapy, no one quite knows how it works. It is not merely a question of giving each of eight people individual therapy while the others listen. There is something about 'groupishness' itself which is curative, but exactly what it is is yet to be discovered."[3]

This group feeling helps people discuss their weaknesses or fears without feeling blamed. It is a feeling of safety and intimacy, and it is sometimes a feeling of indescribable warmth and beauty.

ADMITTING SOMEONE NEW TO THE GROUP

After the group feeling has started to develop, the decision to admit a new member should not be taken lightly, but should be made by the students as a group. There definitely are times to say no. Suppose a class made up of teachers at one school has progressed to the point of being a group, when their principal decides that he would like to join. Letting him in might destroy everything the group had built.

SUPPORT AND SUPPORTIVENESS

To achieve a group feeling, the members of the group should accept and try to help one another. This is "support" in the best sense of the word. One of the cultish outgrowths of the sensitivity movement, however, has been the "supportive" way of treating people. The word "supportive" is used by people such as Carl Rogers with sincerity and understanding, but it has been perverted by others into a kind of euphemism for flattery. Eric Berne, in writing about transactional analysis, warns against this kind of phony supportiveness.

> From the transactional point of view, supportive therapy is regarded as intrinsically spurious. Parental supportive statements (known colloquially as 'throwing marshmallows' or 'gumdrops') are fundamentally patronizing. . . . They can be translated . . . as follows: (1) 'I am glad to have an opportunity to patronize you; it makes me feel worthwhile' or (2) 'Don't bother me with your troubles; take this marshmallow and keep quiet so I can talk about mine.' "[4]

Berne adds "The essence of 'supportive' statements is best shown in a cartoon from *The New Yorker* showing two frogs, one saying to the other: 'Don't be silly, you're no worse looking than any other frog.' "

The incident described above in which Howard revealed his feelings of inferiority, brought forth no spurious "supportiveness."

Nobody said, "You don't really look like Fat Albert," which would have destroyed the integrity of the discussion. The class supported him by accepting with interest what he said about himself. They did not hold his revelations against him, and they did not ridicule him. Later, they helped him overcome his fears by supporting him as their leader, rather than reminding him of his earlier social ineptitude. They even stopped calling him Fat Albert, except for occasional slips.

THE BASIC QUESTION

The basic question explored by the students in these improvised relationships is: How do we relate to each other?

The relationship between Doug and the rest of the class provides an example of how the students answered this basic question non-judgmentally, and at the same time learned something valuable about successful relationships.

Doug was annoyingly manipulative. Almost everyone found him phony and hard to take. In improvisational drama he seemed to learn that his manipulating was not subtle enough. He tried, with some success, to become more skillful at manipulating. Doug's attempts to butter up and deceive people often upset his classmates, and sometimes disrupted class activities. But as the semester went on, the other boys learned how to resist him, and he lost most of his ability to dominate the class. In learning how to parry a manipulator, probably the other boys benefited more from Doug's activities in the class than he did.

As students begin to analyze how they give and take in situations with other people, they learn how to develop more nearly authentic relationships. When a student learns to perceive and understand his own emotions and to relate them to the emotions of other people, he gains in the ability to predict and control his own actions and to empathize with the actions of others. If this process produces changed behavior, it is because the person's perception of himself has changed, not because change was required or requested by the teacher.

Improving human perception seems to be the best way of changing human behavior; advice, admonition, and punishment are of little use. To help students learn about relationships, the teacher should structure the class so that students can share experience without fear of judgment. Carl Rogers describes the desirable climate:

If I am truly open to the way life is experienced by another person—if I can take his world into mine—then I run the risk of seeing life in his way, of being changed myself, and we all resist change. So we tend to view this other person's world only in our terms, not in his. We analyze and evaluate it. We do not understand it. But when someone understands how it feels and seems to be me, without wanting to analyze or judge me, then I can blossom and grow in that climate.[5]

NOTES

1. R. D. Laing, *The Politics of Experience* (New York: Ballantine Books, 1967), pp. 18-19.

2. Erich Fromm, "The Creative Attitude," in *Creativity and Its Cultivation,* ed. Harold H. Anderson (New York: Harper & Row, 1959), p. 46.

3. Eric Berne, *A Layman's Guide to Psychiatry and Psychoanalysis* (New York: Grove Press, 1968), p. 247.

4. Eric Berne, *Principles of Group Treatment* (New York: Oxford University Press, 1966), pp. 314-15.

5. Carl Rogers and Harry Stevens, *Person to Person: The Problem of Being Human* (Berkeley, Calif.: Real People Press, 1967), p. 93.

Ten:
IMPROVISATIONS

The essence of improvisation and characterization is that the actors must create spontaneously. Because the actors have little chance to intellectualize and give the "right" response, they are more likely to be honest about what they really feel or think. By the way he designs improvisations, the teacher can increase the likelihood that students will be exploring in areas that are germane to their lives. Improvisations should not be designed to elicit a predetermined response. Instead, they should stimulate students to deal spontaneously with their real thoughts and feelings.

KINDS OF IMPROVISATIONS

Improvisations may be divided into five main categories:

1. Individual tasks. The actor is put on the stage alone and given a specific task, such as, "Read a newspaper," or, "It is night. You are walking along a deserted street. You think someone is following you."

In these exercises the actor must rely on his own creativity and believability, with neither the support of nor responsibility for interacting with another person.

2. Interpersonal situations. Two or more actors are put on the stage, each with his own task to accomplish. The tasks are designed so that each actor affects the performance of the others. For example, one actor might be told to read a newspaper, while another actor is assigned to read over his shoulder. The situations are designed to stimulate spontaneous reactions.

3. Single characters. A student is given a character to play, with minimal instructions, such as, "Be a teacher," "Be a father," "Be a cop." He is not told how to play it, for he is to provide the content.

4. Characters in situations. In these improvisations, each actor is assigned a character and an emotionally involving task. For example, "You are a young man who is trying to avoid the draft, and you are his brother. You are a sergeant, just entering your family's house after getting home on leave from combat duty in Viet Nam."

5. Abstract improvisations. The teacher throws out a word or phrase, such as "anger" or "cruel." The actor or actors must decide what to do with the concept. Usually they will devise a characterization or situation to make the abstraction concrete.

PLANNING IMPROVISATIONS: VARIATIONS ON THE THEME

In planning improvisations, it is frequently helpful for the teacher to think over several questions about each student after each class: What did he say or do today? What did he seem to be feeling? What interests him most intensely? What seems to be impairing the openness and honesty of his responses?

The most successful improvisations are those done entirely by the students. The teacher simply puts a student or students on the stage and tells them to decide what to do. Relying on this tactic too frequently, however, puts excessive pressure on the students, which may result in stereotyped role playing.

The unpredictability and complexity of improvisations with more than one person means that opportunities for learning are unlimited. But the teacher can enrich the experience even more by varying his instructions. For example, instead of saying, "Play a father," he might say, "Play a father who is different from any father you know." Or he might employ such devices as the role-reversal technique, in which the teacher freezes the improvisation and instructs the two actors to switch roles. This technique can help students broaden their perceptions of other people and develop empathy. However, since reversing roles is most effective if the actors are taken by surprise, it should be used rather sparingly.

Another enrichment technique is to allow a student to choose other people to help him in an improvisation. Or the teacher may instruct the audience that the stage is open to anyone who wishes to help the actor.

Time projection improvisations are very effective in allowing students to express important memories or wishes. They may be told that they can move backward in time to any previous event, forward to something they fear or hope for, or either forward or backward. The instructions might be any of the following:

"Think of the time in your life that you would most like to go back to. Recreate that time. It can be the time of your life that you would like to stay at permanently, or that had the greatest influence on you, or when you first acquired the fear that bothers you the most now, or whenever you like."
"What do you think will be the deciding event in your future?"
"What will your future be?"
"What do you most look forward to (or dread) in your future?"

If the teacher remains keenly aware of his students, and has confidence in them and in his own imagination, he will be able to design improvisations that afford students rich opportunities for discovery and for freeing themselves.

Eleven:
DISCUSSION

It is an illuminating experience for a teacher to walk into a new classroom, introduce himself, and say to the students, "If you know how you feel right now, raise your hand." Most would raise their hands hesitantly, or not at all. They would probably think, with some confusion, "How am I supposed to feel? How does this grown-up want me to feel? What is the right answer?"

When a teacher at the Aspen, Colorado Community School tried this experiment, only a few hands straggled up. Like most twelve- to fifteen-year-olds, this class had been heavily conditioned by years in public schools. In the discussion that followed, the teacher finally asked, "Is there anyone who can know better how you feel than you do?" This time they were sure they knew the answer. "You do!" they chorused.

Within a few months after they start the first grade, most children have learned that if an adult asks a question he already knows the answer, and the child is to give him the answer he wants. Until the pupils are freed from this constricting attitude, the teacher should not pitch into discussions as he would with other adults, but should be content to structure the discussion and help it move along with open-ended questions. Above all, the teacher should strive to overcome the culturally-instilled conviction that he must constantly be teaching.

Harve, a social science teacher who participated as a regular student in a class of boys, got some pointed lessons in nonteaching during the course. Harve was in a difficult position because in absentminded moments his aura of adult authority easily overwhelmed some of the kids. That happened early in the course during the discussion after an improvisation by Carole, the only other adult member of the class.

Carole's improvisation started when George handed her a telephone and told her to be angry. Sitting on the floor in the spotlight, she began a conversation with someone at a laundry about the fact that her clothes were a week late. Her voice and face expressed annoyance and mild frustration.

When Carole was finished, George asked, "Did she accomplish her task? Was she angry?" The answer was a mixture of yeses and nos. Harve's yes was one of the loudest, while Robby yelled a loud no.

Harve said, "She was angry but she was polite about it."

Doug added, "I think she was trying to blackmail this guy. She said he did cleaning for four other people she knew, and if he didn't get over there and take care of her cleaning she was going to tell those people."

George turned to Robby, who looked withdrawn and seemed to have lost confidence in his original opinion. "What do you say, Robby?" Robby muttered, "I don't know."

George asked, "What do you mean?" "She was angry," Robby whispered.

George said, "Robby, just because he says it, and he says it, and he says it, doesn't mean that what you think isn't important. What do you think? It *is* important." Robby sat looking at the floor until George, suppressing a bit of anger himself, said, "Harve can be wrong, baby!" Robby looked up quickly and said, "Well, when everybody else went up on stage, when they were angry, they had an angry look on their face. Carole talked and she was angry, but her face didn't look like she was angry."

"What does an angry face look like?" Harve asked Socratically. "Is there only one way to look angry?"

"No," Robby mumbled.

George said, "Talk up, Robby. Go ahead."

Robby said "I didn't feel that she was angry," and he drew back as if that was all he had to say. But George persisted, "Why?"

"I don't know. She didn't look like she was really angry. Usually when you're angry, you sweat and everything else."

"Any other feelings?" said George.

"She was really good," Harve said "supportively." "She was rubbing her forehead and her voice sounded irritated. It was the kind of situation where she was not screaming mad."

"Was she angry, or annoyed?" asked George. Some boys called out "angry" and some said "annoyed."

"I think she was angry, but in control of it," Harve said approvingly. "She wasn't going to blow her stack."

After the class, George questioned Harve about his persistent "teaching." Harve explained that he had thought it very important for the kids to recognize that Carole had showed well-controlled anger, and he had been trying to explain in depth what was going on.

With all the patience he could muster, George pointed out, "Your insistence on explaining means that you were not willing to let the experience stand for itself. The kids have some understanding of the experience and its implications; if they don't understand everything, it's because they're not ready. It's not necessary to explain—it's the experience, not the teacher, that enables them to understand."

Harve got the point. But George's explanation was probably less important than the fact that Robby and some of the other boys had hesitated to express their opinions because Harve had been so assured and insistent about his. Harve later wrote in his journal that this experience was one of the most important in his development as a teacher.

WHY TALK ABOUT IT?

We are convinced that students could get quite a lot out of an improvisational drama course with no discussion at all. On any given day the depth and productiveness of discussions often seems to be inversely related to the quality of everything else in the class. When a class is stimulating from beginning to end, everything goes smoothly, all of the acting is good, and each experience is important or moving, the discussions are likely to be brief and lacking in impetus. Although the students are learning a great deal, they have little need to talk about it. But when the class is ragged and the improvisations do not click, the students are likely to work hard at discussion. This is particularly evident when a student-directed class goes badly. These classes often produce some of the most earnest and open discussions, provided the students have opened up sufficiently in the earlier phases of the course.

The value of discussion varies according to the ages and backgrounds of the students. Many a middle-school child has never felt that he was making a valuable contribution to a conversation. When he finds that he can say something of value, and that the other people in the class listen to him, the shy or uncertain student frequently feels better about himself. In addition, the fact that the class often disagrees on what has happened in an improvisation allows the students to learn about the differences in how people perceive things.

A CLIMATE FOR FREE EXPRESSION

The climate necessary for dramatic and physical expression, as well as open discussion, is quite different from that found in most classrooms. The atmosphere should be free of judgment, censoriousness, or reproach, and there should be no suggestion of what the teacher would like students to do, say, or feel. The teacher should seldom give advice, because students quickly come to depend on advice from the teacher and may give up the effort to become maturely independent.

When the students try to force the teacher to make a judgment he should avoid doing so, unless the class has reached the point where his opinion is not given inordinate weight. With any group, the teacher should not offer his opinion until most of the people in the group have expressed their opinions and can listen to the teacher without feeling that he is "telling the answer."

One way to avoid stating an opinion is to answer a student's question with a question. Since frequent use of this device may annoy the students, the teacher should occasionally simply explain that he sometimes keeps his opinions to himself so that the class can make its own discoveries and form its own opinions.

STRUCTURING DISCUSSIONS

Even though most of the talking should be done by the students, the teacher is still responsible for getting the discussion started and encouraging the students to explain themselves more fully.

When an improvisation ends we often ask the actors to sit on the stage and not to speak until everyone else who wants to talk has had a turn. This prevents the discussion from dragging on into argument and self-justification.

The teacher might start the discussion with simple, open-ended questions, such as, "Well?" or, "What happened?" Or he might call out something like, "Okay, let's discuss it."

More specific opening questions might be: Did they accomplish their task? Did his movements seem free? Was he concentrating? Did you believe it? What kind of relationship did they have?

Discussion should be voluntary. Reluctant students should not be forced to talk; they will almost certainly open up as the course progresses.

Eventually the teacher can take a seat with the audience and wait for the discussion to start, rather than prompting with questions. There may be a period of silence, but soon the students will begin to converse among themselves. One of the signs of a good discussion is that students speak to and look at each other without constantly referring to the teacher. There are several ways in which the teacher can encourage this conversational pattern. When a speaker persists in looking at him, the teacher can look elsewhere. Looking at other students in the class encourages the student who is talking to look at them too. Or the teacher might suggest that the student speak to the whole class.

To refocus the attention of a student who is not listening, the teacher should establish eye contact and then shift his eyes to the speaker. By using such physical cues as posture and eye contact to show a keen interest in what every student says, the teacher can help to prevent silly talk and showing off.

The discussion should be stopped, and the next activity started, just before the talk becomes boring or meaningless.

ENCOURAGING FULLER DISCUSSION

With open-ended questions, the teacher can often lead a student to clarify and elaborate on a statement. But these questions should only lead, never force, and the teacher should not be concerned if a line of discussion dies from lack of interesting contributions.

Sometimes a student will make an acutely revelatory personal statement and then quickly draw back as if afraid to go deeper. Unless the teacher is sensitive enough to notice this withdrawal and encourages the student to pursue the thought, the most important part will go unsaid.

The following incident, which occurred in a class taught by a teacher new to improvisational drama, illustrates how easy it is not to hear important cues. In this class, a shy black boy was put on stage and instructed to show fear. As the boy cowered, the teacher said, "If anyone wants to help him, you may." Immediately another black boy, who had seemed hostile even in the warm-ups, stomped onto the stage like Frankenstein's monster. He pursued the other boy until he caught him, and then pretended to choke him to death. With an embarrassed grin, the teacher froze the scene. He later confirmed that he had felt futile because the improvisation had turned into a childish monster game, which seemed to indicate that at least one of the boys had not understood the instructions.

As soon as the actors were seated, a student called out, "He wasn't helping him." Then a black friend of the "monster" said, "Maybe he try to put him out of his misery by killing him!" "To be alive; is that misery?" the teacher asked. With great intensity, the "monster" said, "To some people it is." But the teacher did not hear that last comment. He was getting to his feet to start something else that might work out "better."

Before class, the teacher had told us that his students were very poor in discussions. He had been trying to overcome this problem with intensive verbal warm-ups each day. But verbal warm-ups have limited effectiveness. This teacher needed to work on his own perceptual ability. He needed to learn to listen carefully and patiently to the kids, rather than thinking about his own next move as the teacher.

Twelve:
ENDINGS

We try to give each class an ending that will wrap things up and prepare the students for their next class. Our golden rule is: Send your students unto their next class as you would have them sent unto you. This means that they should be in a positive, upbeat mood, with emotions under control.

After a very active class, or one that has been emotionally frustrating, we try to calm the students through positive, relaxed exercises. If the students are left worried or depressed by what has taken place, then we try to use joyful closing activities. The proper ending can also make a student who has had a rough time during the class feel accepted and at peace with the group.

Of course, the teacher usually chooses his ending extemporaneously when he sees where the students are a few minutes before the end of class, but he should already have thought about alternative endings for different purposes. Moreover, in timing the class, he should be sure to leave time at the end for an adequate resolution.

Students usually understand what the teacher is doing, appreciate it, and try to make the ending effective.

Near the end of a typical class, George realized that the students were flying high. If he did nothing to help them gain control of themselves, their high-strung energies might explode in the halls or their next class. The situation called for a fairly complicated ending.

"Everybody in the pool," George called. The students had done this exercise in warm-ups, and they flopped onto their stomachs on the floor. "Start swimming, slowly and steadily. Now, swim faster. Faster. Much faster. You're in a race. You've got to beat the person next to you. Now, on your backs." The students went through the same acceleration with the back stroke, then on their stomachs again—faster and faster until they started to groan. When he heard the groans, George said, "On your backs. Float. Keep your head out of the water, and keep floating. Relax completely in the water. Breath easily. Feel the water all over your body except your face. It's very relaxing. Feel the water all over you. Relax. Relax more."

When the class was completely still, George flicked on the lights and said, "See you tomorrow."

Had the students been overaggressive but with less nervous energy, a shorter version of this ending might have sufficed. They might have been instructed to fall into an imaginary pool of water and float, or to become leaves floating in a breeze to the accompaniment of relaxing music. Or George might have instructed them to be alone in a room and to simply concentrate on their isolation.

If the students had been even higher, and George had foreseen real trouble for the teacher of their next class, he might have helped them calm down by having them isolate and relax parts of their bodies.

Occasionally George instructed the students to concentrate on their next class, with such directions as, "Put yourself in the mood for your next class. Think about how you want to act in your next class." If a teacher wanted to work intensively on the students' behavior in the following class, he could give the students a minute or two to think about it, and then tell them, "Everybody up and act it out. Act out the way you will be in your next class. Now, think of an alternative way that you could be in that class. Think of a different way, perhaps a way that you would rather be."

If the class activities have been quiet, or if some of the students have become tense and need physical release, the physically involving and freeing exercises are best. We often end classes with dancing, in which the teacher emphasizes moving to the music and moving big. Clapping and shouting often break out during this final dance. In a pleasant variation, the students join hands and dance in a snakelike pattern around the stage and out the door. This ending can produce a lovely group feeling.

When a student has been confronted with personal dislike during a class, or has other reason to feel that he has had a bad time, he should be brought back into the group in some special way at the end of the class. For example, he might be called on to lead the dancing.

A brief ending that we often use begins when the teacher tells one student to put his hand on the floor in the center of the spotlight. If a student has had a hard time in class, he may be chosen to put his hand down first. Then the other students put their hands on top. The teacher instructs them to raise their hands as high as they can, all together at first. Then they strain to reach upward individually, their bodies packed together in the spotlight, until the teacher snaps on the light and ends the class with, "Thank you, and I'll see you tomorrow."

Thirteen:
PUTTING IT
ALL TOGETHER

TAKING CUES FROM KIDS

Classes that have not been thought through and planned beforehand have a high mortality rate. Paradoxically, however, the success of the class also depends on the teacher's picking up cues and changing his plans as he goes along, making the class more relevant to the concerns of the students.

Careful planning helps the teacher clarify his purpose and prepares him to react quickly—almost instinctively—to situations as they arise, to pick up a cue and instantly make imaginative use of it.

One day Pat and Robby came into the classroom red faced and panting from one of those spontaneous between-class fights whose seriousness is ambiguous to spectators and participants alike. George welcomed them to the class. He had just finished warming up with some dance exercises, preparing himself mentally, emotionally, and physically to project vitality throughout the class.

As always, he had memorized his lesson plan and alternatives so he would not have to interrupt the flow of the class by consulting his notes. Of course the plans did not take into account the boys' fight or any other spontaneous interchange that would happen that day. Jellyroll Jones was leading the warm-ups, and George was one of the students during the first segment of the class.

The day before this class, Jellyroll had showed his written plan to George, and they had discussed the principles of planning and technique. Why use these exercises? How does one activity lead to another? How does the teacher conduct himself? Jelly, like the other students, was learning to structure group activity. By the end of the semester, every student would have planned and led full classes.

Jelly began the class with a wild dance to Ramsey Lewis's version of "Hard Day's Night," then led the group through fencing drills (using imaginary foils) and other physical activities.

"It's hot in here," Jelly cried. The group "sweltered" in an exercise stressing concentration and believability. Then the temperature plummeted and it was very cold. The shivering boys clustered together on the floor to share their body heat. Frank huddled close to Jellyroll, who had been experimenting with black militancy. Jellyroll ostentatiously ignored the white boy. Frank was obviously aware of the response to his testing, and slipped around to the other side of the clump to find warmth.

At some time during the semester, such observations might help George in his planning. If his observations are wrong there is no harm done, since he is not going to tell the students what he has observed. Of course, he picks up cues even before the class begins. His observation that Pat and Robby had been fighting might be important in determining how the class will proceed after warm-ups.

After the "freezing" exercise, George took over for the rest of the class. In the first exercise, he tied the left wrist of one boy to the right wrist of another, and instructed them, "You must relate to one another. You must communicate something. But you must not talk."

The assigned task was wide open—the boys had a wide choice of action and characterization. Against a musical background provided by the record player, they became a pair of escaped convicts. Their acting was vigorous and uninhibited. Then George gave the same task to Wilt and Cathy, a blonde Antioch college student who was working in a cooperative program at the Advancement School. They started out with some friendly tugging. As Wilt began to get domineering, Cathy's smile changed to a look of alarm. She offered some resistance, but Wilt continued to drag her around the stage until George called, "Freeze!"

"Everybody in a circle around me," George said. Arms about each other, the whole group gathered on the floor in the circle of the spotlight. Usually the actors do not speak until after the audience has discussed their improvisation. But George said, "This time, let's ask Wilt and Cathy to talk about their improvisation first, then you discuss it among yourselves."

Wilt went first. "We were chained together, and she didn't want to go the same way I did. She kept pulling on the chain."

Cathy responded thoughtfully, "I wasn't sure what the relationship was. I knew that he was trying to do something I didn't want to do, and that he was hurting me. At first I wasn't thinking about two people pulling against each other for any reason. I just thought it was sort of interesting that we were pulling against each other, and then I realized from Wilt that he was taking the part of somebody that was trying to hurt me, and then I started getting scared."

A brief dispute erupted over the quality of the acting, during which Wilt volunteered that he liked to "beat on people."

In a mildly interested, nonjudgmental tone, George asked, "Why?"

"Just to show 'em who's who," Wilt mumbled.

"Just to show 'em who's who. What do you think about that?" George asked.

Wilt said, "I think it's all right. Not really, but in self-defense."

George turned to Frank, who was buzzing excitedly to the boy next to him. "Frank, Wilt just said he likes to beat on people because it shows them who's who. What do you think of that?"

"He's right," Frank said. "Well, he doesn't go round, you know, slugging people."

"In self-defense he'll beat 'em," said Chet.

"In self-defense he'll beat 'em," George repeated.

"But sometimes you have to beat 'em, cause if you don't, they gone get you," Chet said positively.

Wilt agreed. "You have to beat 'em up one time or another, or, like, like you walking down the street; someone, he's mad; he hit you on the head. You gotta punch him. He not mess with you no more."

Frank said, "Yeah, we got this kid around our way—five years older than me. He really beats the crap outa me."

"He beats the crap out of you?" George asked.

"Yeah, sometimes. He did it, but I started to get smart. So one time I went in the house and I got a hammer, you know, one of those nice ones. He came over and started beating me and I walloped him in the face with it." The boys laughed appreciatively.

George said, "Now wait a minute, I've got a very interesting thing I want to try. Let's see if you can do something. Get back to your seats quickly. Concentrate. Relax. This time, let's see if we can do what Wilt was saying. Wilt says you've got to show 'em who's who. Right?"

"Right!" they chorused.

"Right, Wilt?" This time I want to see if somebody can show somebody else who's who *without* . . ."

"Fighting," finished Doug.

Here, George abandoned his own lesson plan in favor of an activity defined by the boys. During the improvisations, in which they were instructed to "relate to one another" and "communicate something," and in the discussions following, the boys had demonstrated that their concern in relating to people was, as Wilt put it, "showing 'em who's who." The phrase, expressed in their terminology, had touched a vital concern of the boys, and they were completely involved in the discussion. George picked up on "who's who," and based the next series of improvisations on this phrase.

To launch the next improvisation, George placed Charles, a withdrawn black boy, in the spotlight with Frank. "Let's see if they can show who's who without fighting," George said. "You may speak."

Frank began, "Look, you're so small, I could punch you down with one fist. You're too wise for a little kid, but I want to tell you something: If I hit you I'd knock you out cold. I'm getting sick of you, you little bitch."

After about two minutes of this, they seemed to have established an unshakable theme. George shook hands with both boys and seated them in the center. The believability of the improvisation was praised by all the boys except Jellyroll, who had been skeptical of nearly everything for several days.

George asked Wilt why he had believed the performance. "Lots of guys does it that way," Wilt said. Frank laughed and said, "Yeah, bullies!" He had enjoyed playing the kind of person he feared and disliked, and the class as a whole had made a primitive addition to its catalog of ways to show who's who.

George asked, "What method were they using? Was there a method here of showing who's who, besides hitting?"

"Yes," Doug said. "He was telling him off."

Then George put Robby and Pat in the spotlight. They had been avoiding each other since their fight before class. By waiting until later in the class to put them on stage together, George made it less obvious that they were being paired partially as a result of the fight.

George's instructions were, "Now this time, same task. You have to show who's who. Only this time, you can't fight, and you can't do what Frank and Charles just did. You have to do something completely different—an alternative. Think about it for a second. Be serious about it. You may talk."

Robby started out. "Small fry."

"Who?" Pat responded.

"You."

"I'm boss around here, man."

"Well, I'm boss."

"You're smaller than me, so I'm boss."

"I don't care, I'm boss."

"Boss of what?"

"Boss of you. That's what."

"Boss of city dump?"

"No."

"If you're not boss of city dump, then what dump are you boss over?"

Robby pointed triumphantly at Pat. "This dump!"

After the exercise, Robby and Pat grinned at each other as they sat together in the spotlight. Each realized that they had been only partially acting. How much they analyzed their feelings would be up to them; if they chose, they could accept the safety of regarding the improvisation as purely theatrical.

Then George chose Jellyroll to do an improvisation with him. The instructions were to show who's who in still a different way. Jellyroll became a tough gang leader and accosted George for being on his turf. "Hey, man, where you goin'?" George played innocent, and repeatedly distracted Jelly with comments about girls, schools, things to do, and questions such as, "Is your gang one of the best?" Finally, Jellyroll walked away, growling, "Never mind. Sorry I axed you."

In the discussion, the boys praised George's glib method. "You took him from boss to little kid," Pat said. By playing a rather silly fellow, George had demonstrated a workable alternative, while avoiding any implication of, "Now I'll show you how it's done."

The fast-moving verbal exercise we call a chain reaction was next. With the class standing in a circle, George said, "You say one thing, make one movement. It goes right around. You don't hesitate. Just keep going. If you can't think of anything, say 'blank.' The next person picks it up." The rapid-fire spontaneity of this exercise produces a wealth of cues for the teacher to use in understanding his students and structuring his classes. And more important, it gives the students a chance for the free expression of themes that may be more fully developed later. In this particular exercise George picked up a hint of racial conflict.

After the chain reaction, George stepped to the center of the circle. "I'm white and you're all black. Go!" With no further instructions, the students circled George. Most of them shouted racial insults. Doug danced about singing repeatedly, "George is a honkie!" "Freeze. This time I'm black and you're all white." As they circled him, the black students were the most vehement. Wilt said, "You look like something that came out of a hind end."

George had decided to deal with racial attitudes and conflicts in this class because, although the group was concerned with power, they had not mentioned the racial aspects of power conflicts. Students are taught to avoid bringing racial matters into the open. We think the teacher is justified in introducing topics that are important to the students but that are likely to be avoided because of their cultural conditioning. Later classes would provide constructive racial experiences. As the students become free enough to be able to explore the forbidden topic later classes can provide extremely constructive experiences.

After the exercise in which George was black and everyone else white, it was time for the ending. At George's instruction, Chet put his hand down directly under the spotlight. The other boys piled around him, pressing their hands onto the pile over his. As one, the stack of hands rose slowly, up toward the light. Bodies packed together, straining and swaying on tiptoe, they stretched toward the light. "Thank you," George called. From the thicket of arms, one of Pat's fell around Robby's shoulders. They strutted out the door.

After the class, one visitor said that when Wilt was talking about "beating up on people," George should have taken the opportunity to teach the boys about being genuinely concerned for other people rather than trying to dominate. "Don't you think people *should* show concern for each other?" he asked. The suggested approach would indeed have taught the boys something—that they were expected to be nice and to hide their aggressive feelings. Certainly the world is well supplied with people who have learned their lessons in just such a manner, and are still making A's. Many of these adults never become perceptive enough to see the gap between their professed beliefs and their destructive actions.

George did not say anything judgmental about the boys' conversation. By not saying, "You should not want to beat on people, Wilt. There are better ways of working things out," he left enough room for the students to explore their own reactions to Wilt's attitude. Improvisational drama is best used to allow students to develop their own perceptions and ability to communicate, not for the teacher to teach them how to be sensitive, or socially acceptable, or whatever the teacher values.

PLANNING FOR TOMORROW

The best time to start planning Tuesday's class is as soon as possible after Monday's. Today's lesson leads to tomorrow's, and George had plenty to think about after the class described above. His immediate concern was, "How do I teach tomorrow's class as an outgrowth of today's?"

An experience with a different class illustrates how this question can be answered constructively by helping the students to become more physically free and to realize what they can do with their bodies. George had begun that class by seating the students in a tight circle on the floor and asking them if they knew what the drama class was all about. They said nothing. Not one student offered a suggestion as to what the class was about. They had not been told, and they had no confidence in their own ability to figure it out. George asked them to think carefully about his question and see if they could discover any answers by the end of the day's class.

Warm-ups began with dance movements, beginning with various parts of the body in isolation and working up to movement of the whole body. After that the class pushed out imaginary walls that were closing in and picked up imaginary rocks, then went back to big dance movement as a group. The warm-ups concluded with concentration on, and physical response to, the statement, "There is no air in this room."

After warm-ups, George put on a record and began to move freely to the music, expressing in movement what he heard. Then he changed the record and brought a student to the center. "React to the music" was the only direction given. After each student had a chance to express himself to a different record came the ending. The group stood in the center of the stage in a big circle and clapped out the rhythm of the music. Finally, they moved to the music by isolating parts of their bodies.

Just before the end of the class, George gathered the boys in a small circle on the stage and asked the same question that he had asked at the beginning: "What was our class all about?" This time the kids responded. "We loosened up." "We weren't scared to get up in front of everybody and dance." "We talk better now than before the class."

In reviewing the class later, George recalled that the kids had done free movements very well, and that their comments indicated understanding. As he thought about where to go next, George realized that although the students were involved in moving freely with the music, they were not concerned with using movement to communicate. Physical freedom to them meant abandon: do anything you want, no need to control it. There was the next day's challenge.

The students needed to learn that they could become even more free by improving their control of their bodies, so George decided to have them be animals the next day. In moving like specific animals, they would have to control their bodies to communicate to others what animal they were; in doing so, they would have the experience of using their freedom meaningfully.

PLANNING FOR INDIVIDUALS

Reviewing a class also brings out ideas for improvisations that will help individual students. One day, George asked the actors to demonstrate, one at a time, "What I don't like about myself." Some played it safe: "I've got to change my study habits," or "I've got to be a better-behaved person." Some were more personal. Either response is acceptable; we never force students to be "deep" or "probing."

When it was his turn to show what he did not like about himself, Robby did a skit which he did not immediately understand. He was a bank robber and the cops were chasing him. He ran from the cops into a doctor's office. He begged the doctor to change his face. He kept pleading with the doctor and got no response. It seemed that the doctor would not help him.

When the improvisation ended and Robby sat down to discuss what had happened—focusing on whether or not he was believable— he kept pulling his sweater up over his pug-nosed face. His classmates dwelt on the fact that he didn't really seem like a bank robber because he didn't carry a gun, and that he didn't really seem scared of the cops because he smiled often. No one mentioned his desire to change his face. No one even remembered that his task was to demonstrate "What I don't like about myself." George kept quiet. If the boys did not understand the significance of the skit, then they were not ready to. After the class, George thought about how he could design an exercise that would help Robby understand his own improvisation, without discussion.

The next day George's instructions for an improvisation were, "Convince someone to give you something of his that you want." The focus was on being convincing, not on what was being asked for. When it was George's turn, he stared into an imaginary mirror. He carefully examined his "reflection" and made belittling, humorous faces at himself. Finally, he spoke to himself. "Oh, what a face. Where did you get that face? Only a mother could love that face on payday. Oh, do something about it."

George turned from the mirror and spoke directly to the class. "Oh, do I need help. Come on, now, who's gonna give me his face. I'm telling you, I need a new one 'cause I met this beautiful girl and I gotta impress her." Stopping in front of Robby, he leaned down and thoughtfully scrutinized his face. "Robby, your face. That's it. I want your face. She'll love me if I look like you. Can I please have your face?"

Robby smiled and said, "Yes."

George persisted. "Oh, really, Robby, you're such a friend. You're such a kind person to let me have your face. Robby, I'm so happy because if I have your face, then I will be handsome and the girls will love me and I won't have any more problems. Okay. You give me your face and I'll give you mine."

Now Robby was not smiling. He had realized what was happening. Here he was being complimented on his face, and at the same time he would have to give it up and get stuck with George's. He interrupted and said, "No, I'll keep my own face."

In the discussion, the boys said George had failed in his task. If he had been convincing, they said, Robby would have swapped faces. No one believed him except Robby, who had learned something. For the next few days, he went out of his way to talk to George whenever he saw him.

We find it helpful for the teacher to write occasional short notes to himself about each student and what seems to be happening to him in the class. This helps the teacher sharpen his awareness so he can build the class around the needs of the students. For example, if the teacher's notes show him that several of the students are consistently quiet or withdrawn, the next day's class might emphasize getting them to speak up. They might be instructed to talk to each other from opposite sides of the stage. Or if a student is frightened, he might be chosen for light-hearted, funny skits that would enable his classmates to enjoy his performances. If the student enjoys what he is doing, he is likely to loosen up and volunteer to talk and act more in class.

PURPOSEFUL FLEXIBILITY

The teacher can usually hold to the purpose he had set for a class even while changing his specific plans. Meaningful shifting is more likely if the teacher has his purpose for the class clearly in mind.

Purposeful flexibility was demonstrated in one class designed to encourage free discussion. George had planned to place the students on stage in pairs and instruct them to show anger, but the discussions after improvisations were stiff, and the students seemed afraid of getting personal with each other after having been together only a few weeks. When the students began to fidget and whisper, George caught his cue to shift gears. These kids were not yet ready to face each other singly and then discuss their interactions with the group.

Understanding that the students felt threatened, George dropped his plans and improvised, but he kept in mind his purpose—encouraging free discussion—and tried to pursue it with a more appropriate design. Half the class became a gang of Indians, and the other half a gang of cowboys. The two groups faced each other across an impenetrable barbwire fence. The assignment was, "You cowboys are to tell these Indians what you don't like about them. And you Indians are to tell these cowboys what *you* don't like about *them*."

Standing in their groups, with the teacher-imposed fence to give them physical safety and force them to make their impact verbally, the students called out complaints and insults to the other group. No individual confrontation was required.

Although this step may seem primitive, it was a step that this particular group was ready to take at that time. The group action was a lower-geared attempt to fulfill the purpose underlying the original plan for the class, and it helped lead the students toward free individual discussion.

The purpose fixed for a class should be open-ended, and concerned with the processes of the course. It should not be a content purpose, such as leading the students to realize the importance of loving humanity. The purpose may involve encouraging the students' skills, by, for example, stimulating conversation in a class that is verbally immature.

WATCH THE SIDELINES TOO

A good teacher must be constantly aware not only of the students at the center of activity at any given moment, but also of those who are peripheral. In improvisational drama, this means watching the audience as well as the actors. Often a student's reaction to what is happening onstage is a clue to what kind of task would be of benefit to him.

Awareness of the students is also essential to a teacher's sense of pacing, which he needs to make the class dynamic and flowing. If the class starts to drag, vitality and concentration give way to boredom and daydreaming. If the observers get restless, they can hinder the actors' ability to concentrate. The improvisation should usually be stopped when the audience gets bored, although there are exceptions.

When a student is uncooperative, or otherwise exhibits anxiety, the teacher might show concern by sitting next to him during part of the class, or placing a hand on his shoulder at some appropriate moment during the class. Even the kind of alienated urban youths we worked with at the Pennsylvania Advancement School rapidly come to trust the teacher as they learn that he is in the class not as an opponent but as someone who cares.

At the start of a class in which he had planned to concentrate on believability, George noticed that there was hostility among three of the boys in the audience. Chet and Wilt repeatedly looked at each other and then glared at Doug, who eyed them like a camel. George surmised that the boys must have had an altercation before class.

George could have plowed on through his lesson plan, pretending that the three boys were getting something from it. This is the method of those teachers whose goal is to be able to report that the students have "covered" the prescribed material, regardless of what they have actually learned during that hour.

These three boys were too preoccupied with each other and with what had happened earlier in the day for anything else to be relevant. Taking the cue, George came up with a different exercise.

"When I bring you onto the stage, you must choose someone you don't know very well, and show that person how you might get to know him better. Or you may choose someone you have had a

disagreement with lately and act out a way to solve that disagreement."

The first choice gave the boys who had no quarrels with their
classmates something to concentrate on, and it gave Doug, Chet, and
Wilt the right to decline to deal with their problem if they chose. The
teacher cannot be sure of the right moment to work out a problem,
and it is impractical and dangerous to try to force students to work
out something they are not ready to handle.

After two improvisations it was Chet's turn. Chet helped Doug
onto the stage, and they began to reenact their argument and explore
it further. The improvised situation was more structured than the
original incident. Their task was to solve the disagreement, and they
could not take the easy way out by resorting to violence. Because
only one boy at a time was allowed to face off with Doug, the
original situation of two against one was eliminated. All of these
factors contributed to the boys' progress. After another improvisation, George put Wilt in the center. He immediately chose Doug to
help him with his task, and the two of them went at it, making still
more progress.

At the end of the class George said only, "Shake somebody's
hand." Chet and Wilt immediately stepped straight toward Doug,
who met them halfway. Each shook his hand.

This particular class—disrupted plans and all—had been more
meaningful than any a teacher could have planned. It was relevant to
the boys because they had been presented with a meaningful choice
of actions, and they had worked on a task that was important to
them. The best thing a teacher can hope to do is to increase the
frequency with which these moments of discovery occur.

Fourteen:
RACIAL CONFLICTS AND
OTHER TABOO SUBJECTS

Although the content of the improvisational drama class is usually provided by the students, there are times when the teacher should push a subject, repeatedly setting up situations in which the group will have to deal with the problem in some way. This should be done only when it becomes apparent that the subject is important to the students, but that they have been conditioned to avoid it.

Two fruitful areas for exploration—despite the discomfort of the students—are racial attitudes and conflicts, and relationships with authority figures such as teachers and parents.

Even though racial issues play an important part in the lives of most Philadelphians, George's first improvisational drama group at the Pennsylvania Advancement School did not mention race during the first month of classes. Racial attitudes obviously influenced some of their actions, but nobody was going to talk about it. When race finally was discussed, it seemed to be possible only because it was one of those days when everybody was loose and with it. When the students were on the stage, they gave their all. When they were seated, they concentrated intently on what the other actors were doing. When discussions started, they were bursting with ideas to share with one another.

Larry was assigned to do an improvisation with a University of Pennsylvania graduate student who was taking the course as part of her teaching internship. They went on a date and played it well. Their performance was not unusually dramatic or interesting, but it was believable.

As the class discussed the believability of the improvisation, Larry said, "I believed what I was doing 'cause I date white girls all the time." The room became quiet. Larry was one of five black boys in the group, and the girl was white.

"Don't you ever date colored girls?" asked Joey, a white boy. The group was extremely quiet.

"No," Larry said. " 'Cause colored girls are all whores."

The group started to laugh. The white boys started laughing first, and the black boys picked it up. Whenever there was comedy, Howard had to get into it. "Yeah, all the colored girls I know are *no-o-o-o* good!" More laughter. When the talk slowed and quieted, George said, "Well, does everyone feel the same way?" The four white boys had not said much. Now Artie said, "It's true. Black girls is all real loose. They'll do anything the first time you take them out."

The discussion continued along this line until George could contain himself no longer. Feeling that Larry would see the absurdity of his generalization if it were brought close to home, George turned to him and said, "Do you have a sister, Larry?" "Yeah." "Well, tell me, is she a whore?" "Yeah, she is. She had to have an abortion when she was fifteen. She's so bad that my daddy has to lock her up in her room so she won't go out and get into more trouble."

After the class, George was shaken. There was more involved here than notions about the social habits of black females; that was only symptomatic. The unanimity of the stereotype was particularly disturbing. Were the black boys trying to please the whites? Was this inevitable as long as the teacher was a white male?

There were other things bothering George. In all of his other classes, the black and white students had been about equally talented and intelligent. In this class all the blacks seemed brighter than any of the whites. From the beginning of the course, however, the black boys had taken a figurative back seat. They agreed with everything the white boys said and did. No white boy's acting ever drew a negative comment from a black boy.

George had been wondering what, if anything, he should do about this. He had been hoping that the condition might cure itself naturally. But the discussion about black girls had brought the situation to a head. If only there had been some disagreement, or they hadn't been so raucously jovial about it, there might have been some hope that the boys would get into the racial problem themselves. Now George saw that he would have to design activities that would lead the boys to bring out their racial feelings and attitudes, explore them, and keep on exploring them, without getting a chance to tuck them safely away again.

Rather than assure the class that some of the finest people he knew were black women, George brought a black Advancement School secretary into the class. The boys played scenes in which they related to her in various ways, such as taking her on a date. For the rest of the course she was a regular student, and a popular one.

Rather than stating that there was a great deal of white supremacist feeling in the class and that they ought to stop feeling that way, George bombarded the boys with one experience after another in which they could get their feelings out. They shouted "nigger" and "white mother fucker" at each other, and the awful secret began to come out in the open. Nearly every day, through improvisations, physical contact, and other exercises, the boys brought their racial feelings into the open. Despite some difficult moments, the change in their racial attitudes soon became evident. By the end of the semester they were able to admit their fears and prejudices, and they could listen without being insulted when a white boy said he was afraid of black boys, or a black boy said he did not like honkies. They had by no means rid themselves of racial dislikes, but they were able to talk openly.

Dick, a boy of Polish origin, was the most overtly prejudiced person in the class. He could hardly stand to look at a Negro, and sometimes became genuinely nauseated in their presence. Dick hated the class for the first week or so. He had a close crewcut, and the long-haired teacher was greatly upsetting to him. About the time he became somewhat reconciled to being in the same room with George and a bunch of black boys, the racial issue surfaced. Dick went through hell for a few days, then said he could not stand to come to the class any more. George told him the choice was his.

A week later, Dick said he wanted to rejoin the class. We never learned the reason for his change of mind; he seemed to be drawn irresistably back into a painful situation. Neither could we pinpoint any particular event that transformed his attitude toward black people or toward George. But the difference gradually appeared in his expression, which changed from sour and withdrawn to relaxed and alert, and in his posture. He started out lying back on his cushion. As the weeks passed his spine straightened a few degrees at a time, and then began to point slightly toward the center of the stage. He became tolerant of George and then openly admired him. And he became able to discuss race and to do race-oriented improvisations with black boys. By the end of the semester, Howard was his best friend.

It was amazing to see Dick in the lunch area, happily eating and talking at a table where all of the other boys were black.

When they have brought some of their racial feelings into the open, classes often get the euphoric feeling that they have achieved perfect brotherhood. They have not. Racial prejudices are varied, complex, subtle, and sometimes ineradicable. But progress can be made, and to ignore and supress these powerful prejudices makes the class an absurd exercise in hypocrisy.

The class described here felt that euphoria. They were sure that they accepted each other as brothers and equals. Although they fell far short of that end, some beneficial changes were apparent. The black boys took the lead in the class, not by grabbing power, but through creative performance. The white boys were stimulated by their black classmates to freer, more imaginative movement and acting. The students were able to free themselves to learn from each other.

GETTING IT OUT IN THE OPEN

In all our Philadelphia classes, there came a time when the cues from the students indicated that we must either bring the racial feelings into the open or forget about developing deeper and more honest relationships in the class. At this point, our usual icebreaker was for George to stand center stage, gather the class around him in a circle, and say, "You're all white, and I'm black."

The kids would circle him. Invariably, all of the black kids and all or most of the white ones would begin shouting racial slurs. Then George would be white and all of the students black. He might switch them back and forth several times.

This exercise was never followed by discussion or by any show of disapproval from George. After it was over, George was still George. He had borne the brunt of it, and the kids had gotten the awful and unspeakable into the open. The students are further protected by the fact that, "It's all an act." It is interesting that the "acting" of all of our Philadelphia groups was so much alike, even though the only instruction given was, "You're all white, and I'm black," or vice versa.

This exercise should be followed by an ending that allows the students to work off some energy and then come together again, such as stacking hands under the spotlight.

The teacher should be very cautious about putting a student in the middle of the circle, even after the class has made progress in dealing with racial conflict. A student in the center should never be regarded as a member of his own race. That is, black boys should only "be" white and white boys only black.

The nature of the insults hurled at the teacher in this exercise was sometimes as surprising as their vehemence and spontaneity. For example, when George was supposed to be black, a couple of the black boys called out, "You look like something that came out of a hind end." There were other insults of this nature, including the time-honored, "Hey, white boy! Who shit on you?"

Although such observations might lead to speculation that American racism contains a substantial element of fecal association, the function of the exercise is not to provoke psychological speculation or cerebral understanding but to desensitize the students enough to open the door to constructive experiences.

PHYSICAL FAMILIARITY

Making physical contact with a person of another race is an enlightening experience for many people. In one class, George paired each white person with a black person for the face feel. The instructions were, "Pretend that you're blind. You don't know what the face of the person opposite you is like. Use your hands to discover what that face is like. Then, very quietly, tell that person some things about his face." After several minutes, George said, "Tell that person how his face is different from yours." Then they switched roles, with the other person in each pair being blind. George gave the boys individual encouragement to really feel each other's faces, especially the lips and nostrils, areas that most people will avoid.

After the exercise, George started the discussion by asking, "Did you find any differences between your faces?" Doug apparently had noticed that each pair had one black person and one white, and, as usual, he tried to give the expected response. "Yes, his face is white. Mine is brown."

"How could you tell that if you were blind?"

"By the hair."

Pat said, "If you were in the Army, they'd cut your hair real short. Then you couldn't tell." Doug laughed raucously. "But seriously," George said, "If my hair were cut very short like Doug's, do you think you would be able to tell the difference?"

The group was seated in a tight circle. Pat rose to his knees and

carefully studied Wilt's hair. As they discussed the problem incon-
clusively, Jellyroll took a lock of Ray's blond hair between his fingers and rubbed it delicately. Ray, in the meantime, was brushing his
fingertips across the top of Chet's natural.

"At the bottom, Jellyroll's face is wide," Robby said. "His nose is
flat. Mine ain't flat." The conversation trailed off as the boys flopped
across the pile of bodies one way and another, totally involved in
feeling different kinds of hair and faces. Eventually they broke it up
for an ending exercise, but as the boys walked out the door, Jellyroll
Jones once again was fingering Ray's hair and studying it intently.

RACIAL ASPECTS OF ACTIVITIES

After the class has done the circling-the-teacher exercise a few
times, the issue of race may be raised again with the tug-of-war. In
this believability exercise, two teams have a tug-of-war first with a
real rope, and then with an imaginary one.

The boys in this particular class were unusually nice, and rather
dull. After they had done the tug-of-war with racially mixed teams,
George said, "Blacks on one side, whites on the other." The boys
were stunned. With little cries of protest, they stopped and stared at
George. He gave them the instructions again, and, with the blacks
on one side and whites on the other, they repeated the tug-of-war.
Their nervousness was evident throughout the exercise.

In the discussion the next day, most of the boys told George very
earnestly that they should not have exercises pitting the races against
each other. "Why not?" George asked. Because, they admitted with
clear understanding, they were always fairly close to having a fight
break out between the races anyway. Having made this admission,
the boys were ready to go on and deal with their racial conflicts.

The "fence" exercise can also have racial implications. In this
exercise, an imaginary high fence divides the group in half, with a
racially mixed group on either side. At first, one group is labeled
cowboys and the other Indians. After they have threatened and insulted each other for a little while, the labels are changed so that one
side is black and one white. After a minute or two, each side switches
race.

EXPLORING RACIAL ATTITUDES AND RELATIONS

Racial Coaching

When the students are able to deal with racial differences without blowing sky high, they are ready for a fascinating exercise in which they are paired, with one black person and one white in each pair. The instruction is, "Each of you who is black is to teach your partner how to be black." After giving them ample time for coaching, the teacher calls them back to their seats. Then each white student is given a turn on the stage to "be black." His black partner is also brought onto stage to be his coach.

After the discussion, the teacher spreads the students out again, in either the same black-white partnerships or new ones, and tells the whites to teach the blacks how to be white. Each black student then has a chance to show what he has learned, with his white partner coaching him. The exercise can be often continued with blacks teaching whites how to be white, and whites teaching blacks how to be black.

The discussions of this exercise are always vigorous and interesting, as the students challenge one another's stereotypes in the context of talking about how well they carried out their tasks.

A Class Stressing Race

After warm-ups stressing vigorous movement and relaxation, George brought Jellyroll and Robby onto the stage and instructed them, "Look at each other. Jelly, you're white. Robby, you're black. I want you to work hard to try to believe it." Then George took his seat, leaving the two boys standing there.

Spontaneously, Robby yelled, "Hey, white boy! Whatchoo doin' around here?"

"Just walking," Jellyroll said politely.

"Hanh, hah!" Robby sneered. "Well, this is our turn, see? The black people's turn! Get it?" As Robby continued to bully him, Jellyroll minced stiffly about, occasionally giving brief, polite answers.

In the next improvisation, Pat was black and Wilt was white. Wilt quickly accepted Pat as his friend. As they were talking, George sent Doug, who was black, onto the stage as a white boy. "Say, man,"

Doug said to Wilt. "You gonna let that nigger hang around with you?"

"We're friends, man," Pat told him.

"Ooooh," said Doug incredulously.

Pat turned to Wilt. "Ain't we friends, man?"

"Yup," Wilt agreed.

"Well," said Doug, "I don't want to be friends with a colored person."

Wilt defended his "black" friend Pat, and Doug said, "You're 'spozed to be stone white boy, right? And you're goin' to go round with a nigger like that?" Wilt put his arm around the "black" boy and said, "C'mon, Pat. You be my friend." The two of them walked away together, leaving Doug making faces after them.

In the discussion afterwards, Doug said he had been quite sure that Pat was going to lure Wilt down behind the drugstore, where Pat and "a bunch of his colored friends" would "beat up on Wilt." Doug had gotten so involved in his role that by the end of the improvisation the anti-black prejudice he expressed seemed to be quite real.

In the improvisations that followed, in which the task was the same, a great deal of hostility toward white racists was expressed by both white and black actors.

In one improvisation, the two actresses, and some of the spectators, became furious. Carole, a black counselor from another school, who was taking the course as a student, was told only to be white. Cathy, the blond Antioch College cooperative worker, was to be black.

When George said, "Go," Carole forced the corners of her mouth down and walked up to Cathy, eyeing her suspiciously. "Do you work around here?" Carole asked, in a whiny, accusative voice.

"What business is it of yours? It's none of your business whether I work here or not!"

"Well, lady, we just don't have that sort of thing, and . . . now hold on a minute!" She grabbed at Cathy, who said, "You stupid bitch! Keep your hands off me!"

Talking very slowly, in a poor imitation of a Southern accent, Carole said, "We don't have that down heah."

"What don't you have down *heah*?"

"We don't have black bitches down heah walking in certain neighborhoods," Carole said as if lecturing a child.

Cathy was spluttering furiously, but Carole ignored her and continued, "Now this is where *I* live. Now, are you working for someone in this neighborhood?" They paced around like hostile animals. "When I ask for a reply, I want it now. If I have to call my neighbors . . . 'cause we just don't *have* anyone like you walkin' up and down our streets unless they work around heah. You're not going to get off this street without giving me an explanation."

"I wanted to spare you this," Cathy said. "But since you insist—your husband called me up. He asked me to come here."

"My husband couldn't service a ninety-year-old," Carole exploded.

Both women expressed anger that became quite real, and both aimed it at the same character: the white woman played by Carole. Cathy did it directly, and Carole released her anger through an unsympathetic portrayal of the character.

For the next series of improvisations in this class, George instructed the group, "We're now our own race again. This time, you must think of a situation that you've been in where you've been uncomfortable because of your color. In other words, was there a time when you were white and something happened because of it, or you were black and something happened because of it?"

Pat, the first to go on the stage, chose Frank to help him. Both were white. They improvised walking to Connie Mack Stadium at night. The stadium was in the North Philadelphia ghetto, and both boys showed apprehension as they walked past an imaginary group of black men. "I don't like this," Frank said. They were chased, cornered, and escaped. When they finally got to the stadium, they stepped up to the ticket window, where Frank said, "Two tickets to the Nina Simone concert, please."

After a few improvisations based on the same instructions, the group had a long and interesting discussion. They started out by concluding, from the improvisations they had done, that they regarded white people and black people as enemies. They went on to discuss some aspects of racial hostility.

At the end of the class, the boys walked around George while he was alternately white and then black. Then he instructed them, "I want you to dance freer than you ever have before." A racial focus will always cause tension in the students, so the ending should give them ample opportunity to let off steam.

FEAR OF RACIAL CONFLICT

As a group becomes more open about race relations, it usually passes through a second phase of fearing the topic. At this time, students show signs of wanting to withdraw, and often they are quite explicit about it. This particular group reached a crisis point four days after the class described above.

After some improvisations that had nothing to do with race, George said, "When I bring you on the stage, you are to improvise on the advantages of being black or being white. For example, what can a black man do that a white man can't do?" Wilt laughed raucously. "Or what can a white man do that a black man can't do?"

George brought Jellyroll onto stage. "Roll is going to show the advantages of being black." Jellyroll stopped an imaginary person and said, "Hey, boy! C'mere. Where you going?" He grabbed the man and beat him brutally, knocked him down, stomped him and stabbed him, then picked him up and hit him some more. As Jellyroll held the limp form against the wall, pounding away at its head with his fist, George called, "Freeze."

"Let him drop," George said.

George draped an arm around Jellyroll's shoulders and the two of them sat down in the middle for the discussion. The discussion was animated and somewhat hostile. Jellyroll would not say what advantages he saw in beating up people, and some of the boys were upset that improvisations about race always seemed to involve fighting.

After the discussion was broken by a fire drill, George asked, "Now, should I change the topic, or should we stick with the one we have?" The replies were mixed, and someone suggested, "Let's do a group thing." George agreed, and gave the instruction, "We're going to try painting pictures with our bodies. I'm going to call out a word. As soon as you hear the word, figure out what you want to say. Don't say it, but express it through your body."

The students acted out their responses to the words *kindness, school,* and *summer,* and then George called out, "Black." Doug skipped across the room and jumped on Ray. Frank drew his fist back and threatened Doug. "Relax," instructed George. "Get back to your places. The word is *white.*" Again Doug jumped on Ray. This time Frank ignored him and slumped disgustedly to the floor.

Chet said, "Hey, George, man, I don't think anybody likes these problems about race." "All right," George said. "Let's sit down and talk about it, shall we?"

All the boys were talking at once as they sat down. Most said they wanted to avoid race. A few said they liked the topic, and some expressed fear that racial conflict would spread outside the classroom.

After some discussion, the boys turned to George for his opinion. George said, "I think that at times it's probably uncomfortable to discuss racial issues or to do improvisations about race. But I feel that until the time comes when we can discuss it openly, it's still going to be a problem whether we admit it or not. I think that if we can open up and get it out and discuss it, then we can get rid of some of our prejudice."

Carole said, "I don't know that I want it to stop, but I do get disturbed by the violence. It seems that there is nearly always violence when we portray relationships between black people and white people."

Frank, who had withdrawn behind the group to lie down, now put in, "Yeah, like, at the end sometimes we have you in the middle, and you know—'I'm black and you're all white'—well, I don't see why they have to say, 'You look like something that comes out of my ass.' I don't see why they have to say that."

"But people do say it, don't they?" George said. "I never do," Harve protested.

"The reason they call you so many bad names is you don't stop it," Wilt told George.

"He never tells us we have to call him bad names or anything He just says that he's white and we're black, or he's black and we're white," Harve pointed out. "We should stop calling him names, then," Wilt said.

At this point the students were talking much more freely than they had at the start of the discussion. In protesting against consideration of racial matters, they had plunged into the most open discussion of race they had yet had.

After some more discussion of whether to stop considering race in class, George asked, "How about it? Do we do away with race, or not?" The replies were still mixed, but the majority favored continuing to deal with race.

Chet suggested, "Do something like have a black person and a white person tell why they like each other, or something like that."

"What was the improvisation today?" George asked. Several of the boys called out that it was to show the advantages of being black or of being white. George asked, "Did I say to do anything bad?" There was a chorus of noes. "You just said do it."

The students never did get themselves together enough to make a decision on whether to continue dealing with racial matters. But they had come to their crisis point and had brought their racial fears more into the open. Most of them had understood that the hostility brought out in the race-related exercises was their own; it had not been required by their instructions. From understanding, at least partially, that the hostility was theirs, they went on to more positive ways of working out their relationships with each other.

Once a group has come through its crisis, racial matters should be treated as just another way of exploring relationships. Improvisations might be done on such themes as discussions between a Black Muslim and a moderate black, a black boy getting on a bus with a white driver, a black customer and a white store clerk, and so on.

A final note of warning: the teacher cannot help his students deal with their fears about racial issues until he has dealt with his own. Before undertaking to structure an exploration of racial conflict, a teacher should make an inventory of his own fears and decide whether he will be able to follow through. Once a class has been encouraged to bring their racial feelings into the open, it is probably impossible and certainly harmful for the teacher to attempt to cut them off.

Fifteen:
THE STUDENTS
TAKE OVER

In improvisational drama classes there is no call for a student revolution. The students do not need to overthrow a teacher who, from the beginning of the course, watches for the time when they can run their own classes.

The benefits of using students as teachers in academic classes, as well as in improvisational drama, are quite noticeable. The student-teacher gains confidence in himself and a sense of responsibility. He gets to see a reflection of himself as a leader. Classmates often exert themselves to make their fellow students look good as teachers. The group is bound to relate to someone of the same age differently from the way they relate to an adult; this can be a refreshing change for the class, and students often learn things from a peer that they would not learn from an adult teacher. A student who has had experience as a teacher is likely to have greater empathy for his own teachers. The student-teacher often chooses improvisations related to his own problems, so that he gets to see how other people react to and handle things that concern him. And being a teacher and helping other people to have meaningful experiences can be rewarding.

Because of its frequently repetitive structure, improvisational drama is well suited to giving students the experience of teaching. The teacher can start assigning students to lead warm-ups when they seem reasonably comfortable with the structure and with each other. At first the student should be given a few days in which to prepare, and the teacher should participate enthusiastically in the student-led warm-ups.

After most or all of the students have led the warm-ups the teacher can start assigning students or pairs of students to lead whole classes. If two students lead a class together, they can help each other with the planning, boost each other's confidence, and take turns leading different parts of the class.

In the first few classes run entirely by students, the teacher would do well to stay on the sidelines rather than participate as a student. A statement such as "It's your class. I'm not here today," lets the group know that the responsibility is theirs.

Should the class get chaotic or run into trouble, the probable best bet for the teacher is to sit tight and do nothing. After the students take over, they have to work out their own problems. In most classes, the students will cooperate intensely. When the responsibility is theirs, they want to make it work.

In turning the class over to the students, the teacher may indicate that activities will end five minutes before the period is over. Then, in the last five minutes, he can step in and help discuss the processes and structure of what has happened, being careful not to make judgments about the class. This five-minute processing should not be used every time; there should be some days when the teacher is removed from the group for the full period.

After the group is accustomed to having classes without the teacher to provide the structure, the teacher might occasionally sit in the class as a student. This is difficult, because the teacher can never really be just another student; he must be careful not to overwhelm the class with his opinions. He must be completely nondirective. If he cannot help being directive or manipulative, he should never be in the class while a student is running it.

INTERPRETING THE MODEL

Whether he wants to be or not, the teacher is always a model for the students. When the students take over the functions of the teacher, many of them use the opportunity to interpret the model: to try to behave as the teacher does, with refinements of their own. This is often a way of testing their interpretations to see if they really do understand the structure and the way the teacher does things.

Chet was one of the first in his group to be assigned to lead a full class. He had started the semester being surly and critical of George's teaching methods. His attitude toward authority reflected the effects of the punitive treatment he had received in the Catholic schools he had attended and, probably, in his family. Often, he had leaned back on his elbows to show disdain for the class, and George had gently drawn him into discussions with respectful questions.

For the last week or so before he was assigned to lead a class, Chet had seemed to mellow. He was much more cooperative and involved in the class, and he had stopped talking about the way a school *ought* to be run, although he had not stated directly that he now approved of George's teaching methods.

When Chet took the stage to lead the class, he led it almost exactly as George had. The startling similarity was far from superficial. Chet actually did help the other boys. While an improvisation was in progress, he would lean forward, his body relaxed but ready to spring to the center when he sensed that the action had run its course.

The discussions, as well as the improvisations, went quite well, but Chet noticed that Ray had been withdrawn throughout the class. In a kindly, genuinely interested voice, Chet asked, "What do you think, Ray?" He succeeded in drawing Ray into the conversation, just as George had encouraged Chet to participate many times before. Thus, Chet showed an appreciation for the way George had drawn him out.

Sixteen:
AN IMPROVISATIONAL
DRAMA COURSE:
HOW IT MIGHT GO

In order to convey a sense of the timing for an improvisational drama course, this chapter traces the week-by-week progress of one class that met for one hour a day, five days a week, for thirteen weeks. Other groups have gone at different rates, taken different tangents, and reached different places. Each group, like each student and each teacher, is different.

Because inner-city, underachieving, junior high school boys like Jellyroll Jones, Wilt, and Ray, tend to need much stimulation to develop verbally, physical freeing was emphasized during the first week and part of the second of this particular class. Since some of the boys objected to dancing, much of the movement at first was athletic: fencing, baseball, swimming, and so on.

To alleviate the fears of the students and let them know that he regarded them as individuals, George made sure to sit next to each boy at one time or another and made individual contact in other ways. The boys did shadow play and other exercises intended to focus their concentration outside themselves, to lessen their self-consciousness and allow them to move more easily. In structuring the class, George emphasized vitality, quick pacing, and expansiveness of movement; the bigger their movements, the less likely people are to worry about how they look.

In the second week, the class moved into group verbal exercises. For example, the kids might stand in parallel lines and shout to each other over the sound of loud music. (The body freeing exercises continued throughout the course.)

During the third week, the students were assigned to use their bodies with purposeful control to portray animals and inanimate objects. These exercises required them to think before they moved, and to use their bodies expressively.

By the fourth week, each boy was able to dance to music alone on the stage, interpreting or helping to express the music through movement. They were also doing such verbal improvisations as, "You are on a train. You don't know the person next to you. Try to engage him in conversation." Simple concentration exercises were introduced late in the third week and continued through the fourth. Also in the fourth week physical freeing exercises began to emphasize touch, as in the face feel, sardine can, and telephone booth.

Work on believability started in the fourth week. In the fifth week, believability and concentration were linked and were emphasized equally in improvisations. Also during the fifth week, George began explicitly drawing out racial feelings, with such exercises as "the cage."

By the sixth and seventh weeks, George knew the students quite well, and there was no difficulty in designing appropriate individual improvisations to emphasize relationships between people. These exercises might be as simple as having two students keep rhythm together on drums.

The crisis over whether to continue exploring race or to suppress the topic came in the eighth week. After that storm was past, the boys' improvisations continued to become more expressive. Most of the improvisations by this time grew out of cues given by students. The students also began structuring parts of classes, such as warm-ups, during the eighth and ninth weeks. From the tenth week on, students structured entire classes on about three days each week.

The boys spent their last week together at the Advancement School producing a gaudy commencement show. It seemed important for the group to have a chance to work on a final task after they had learned to work together so well.

Seventeen:
"BUT ... WHAT ARE THEY LEARNING?"

The class was drawing to a close. It had been a good hour, and the boys danced ecstatically to the brazen beat. Prancing and clapping his hands, Jellyroll Jones peered out of the lighted stage area at the sixteen visitors watching from the darkness. Feeling sorry for the left-outs, he danced out of the stage area, and extended his hand to an astonished woman in the audience. She took it and Jelly—still dancing—led her onto the stage.

Robby got the idea as soon as Jellyroll approached the woman. Beaming, he led a stiff-jointed school superintendent onto the stage. Charles, Pat, Doug, Mack, and Wilt followed, as Jellyroll and Robby went back for more visitors. Soon everybody in the room was dancing on the stage, the adults doing their best not to be a drag. Then George took Ray's hand, Ray grabbed Carole's, she grabbed a visitor's, and they all linked in a wavy line. Still dancing, George led them in a snaky pattern out of the classroom and into the hall.

When the boys had scattered, the flushed visitors remained clustered around George, commenting on what they had just witnessed. "The most exciting thing I've seen in education!" "How can *my* teachers learn to do this?"

Then came a familiar question. An iron-haired woman recovered enough from what she had observed and taken part in to pant, "But ... what are they *learning*?"

To try to answer that question, this chapter will describe some of the gains of the students in one class. All were boys from eleven to fourteen years old. All came from Philadelphia public or parochial schools in which they were regarded as not making it; many were potential dropouts. The majority came from families that would be considered poor. Needless to say, some of these boys will wind up lost in the urban jungle. A course at school cannot resolve all of a kid's problems with his family, his neighborhood, his teachers, and the police. But if a student has one important realization in a semester, then the teacher can consider that semester well spent.

ONE GROUP OF BOYS

Ray

When Ray first entered the Pennsylvania Advancement School, he took the Thematic Apperception Test. In a cramped corner of one page, he drew tiny male and female genitalia. After his stay at the Advancement School, during which he took improvisational drama, he took the test again. This time, he filled the page with GREAT BIG male and female genitalia.

One of eleven children in a poor family with a drunken father, Ray had problems that would not be solved in a classroom. From the first, it was obvious that this fine-featured blonde boy was very disturbed. He occasionally volunteered a statement, but if someone spoke to him first he withdrew. His eyes looked dazed, and he acted as unreachable as if he were someplace else.

At the beginning of the course, Ray usually did nothing when he was on stage. He would simply stand there until George came to his rescue. One day Ray was annoying in class, making rude noises during the other boys' improvisations. When George gave Ray an improvisation to do alone, he just stood there, waiting for George to go on stage and either do something with him or show him to his seat. But this time, George just sat and looked at him. Ray's self-consciousness grew until at last George seated him.

After the class, George took Ray across the street to lunch. Over their sandwiches, George said, "You weren't concerned about the other boys when you made noises while they were on stage."

Looking down, Ray said bitterly, "You weren't concerned about me when I was on stage."

"That's only partly right," George said. "I acted like I wasn't concerned about you. Actually, I was. I've been concerned about you ever since our class started. But I acted unconcerned so you could see what it was like."

Ray acknowledged that he got the point. Back in the school building, he told George that he liked him—and that it was the first time he had ever liked a teacher.

For the first half of the semester, the frightened boy always carried some kind of weapon. One day he had a length of chain, which he began swinging during a solo improvisation. When he accidentally hit the wall with it, he threw a quick, apprehensive look at George, who smiled and said, "You may do as you please." Taking a full swing, Ray hit the wall with the chain again, and continued viciously beating the wall until he was exhausted.

Toward the end of the semester Ray was able to express his hostility overtly. This open expression caused him some trouble, but he was well on his way to becoming less withdrawn. He came to mix humor with his hostility quite often. In one class, he did a black-humor improvisation of a drunken man beating his wife and children. It was well done and very funny. Most of the boys were convulsed with laughter, but some of the adult visitors were profoundly horrified.

During this semester, Ray went from hating to be on stage to loving it; from being withdrawn to taking an active part in discussions; from being physically stiff and cold to moving freely and showing considerable vitality; and from being socially isolated to having friends. But there still did not seem to be much chance for him outside.

Wilt

Although he was a strong, handsome boy whose classmates naturally looked to him for leadership, Wilt at first did not seem comfortable as a leader. He seemed to regard himself as a dumb, amiable black boy who needed someone to tell him what to do. For the first few weeks he clung to Chet, sitting next to him, choosing him to do improvisations with, and echoing his opinions.

The other boys particularly admired Wilt for never taking advantage of his size. He never bullied or fought, but consistently acted as peacemaker when other boys squabbled outside the class. During the course of the semester, Wilt came to accept the appreciation of his classmates. He became a leader in the class and in the school. Although Chet remained his friend, Wilt stopped clinging to him and became close friends with other boys of both races.

Wilt was unusually aware of what was happening in the class, and could talk quite perceptively about the ways in which the other boys had changed. He matured substantially during the session, particularly in verbal facility.

Chet

Chet's attitude toward school was negative and fearful. He believed that schools had to be tense places dominated by tyrannical teachers, and that it was better to do nothing than to take a chance on doing something wrong.

As the semester progressed, he began to accept the enthusiasm of his classmates and achieved greater freedom in expressing himself. He became assertive, though not overaggressive, in discussions. Above all, he came to enjoy the course, his classmates, and himself.

Robby

Pug-nosed Robby made extraordinary progress in the course. At the beginning of the semester he was tight, prejudiced against Negroes, and very childish. For nearly half the semester he withdrew from anything that had racial implications. As the course progressed, he became able to accept criticism without sulking. His fear of racial matters seemed to dissipate completely, and he was able to discuss race intelligently. He became much more mature, articulate, perceptive, confident, and assertive.

His first attempts at leading classes went badly, but he later became very good at leading. He became a good friend of nearly every boy in the class, able to demonstrate his sensitivity and concern for other people.

Doug

Doug, a handsome black boy, was seriously disturbed emotionally. He often did not hear people when they talked to him; instead of listening, he seemed to be thinking of how he could manipulate. The group often criticized him in class, although he usually ignored it. On one occasion, however, when he was leading the class, the other boys disliked what he was doing so much that they sat down and protested. Doug announced that he was quitting the course. The next day, he appeared at class time and asked the group if he should stay in the course. The boys said he could stay if he would quit trying to dominate the class. But he heard only the part that said he could stay. Fifteen minutes later he was manipulating again and not noticing his classmates' disgust.

Doug really did not seem able to be honest about anything. His extreme manipulativeness, combined with his better-than-average intelligence, will enable him to avoid getting the intensive professional help that would be his only hope.

Doug probably learned less than anyone else in the class, although he did become smoother about his manipulation. His classmates, however, improved greatly at countering his manipulations.

Charles

Charles was a bright, perceptive black boy who was often paralyzed by distrust of people. On the first day of the course, improvisational drama seemed to capture his fancy, and he did one of the most creative improvisations. But then he withdrew, carrying out the assigned improvisations listlessly and contributing little to the discussions. He was extremely suspicious of the course and the people in it.

Eventually, when he realized that there was no pressure on him to perform, his natural inquisitiveness began to overcome his fear of people. By the tenth week he had developed several close friendships, and one day he ran up behind George in the hall, jumped on his back, and giggled that he wanted a piggyback ride. It was quite a change from his previous extremely withdrawn behavior.

Pat

At the beginning of the course, Pat had a physical complaint every day: a headache, an earache, a pain in his leg. George ignored them. After a few weeks, all the symptoms disappeared. He was trying to develop an identity, and—feeling self-conscious about having no front teeth—seemed on the way to establishing himself as a sort of social monkey on the fringes of the tough guys.

During the course, Pat's self-concept changed substantially. He became able to act or converse seriously and intelligently, and he became sensitive and considerate in his relationships with people. He developed quite a mature attitude toward evaluation of his work. After an improvisation, he might say, "No, that wasn't so good. I didn't believe it." He could do this coolly and analytically, without self-castigation.

Mack

Mack was a large, dark-haired, awkward boy from a middle-class Jewish family. He lacked confidence in his ability to do anything on his own and had trouble looking people in the eye. Although he was about the same size as Wilt, whom he almost hero-worshiped, Mack seemed to think of himself as small and weak. He was terrified of the movement exercises. In the early discussions, he said nothing unless someone asked him a question, to which he would respond, "Ah, uh, I dunno."

Mack made definite strides in gaining assertiveness. He lost his fear of getting on the stage, and became eager to act. By the end of the course he was able to throw himself into dancing with as little inhibition as grace. He was pleased when Wilt returned his friendship and gradually emerged as an energetic, constructive contributor to the group.

Frank

Frank had always used his quick wit to defend himself. In the improvisational drama course, he learned to trust the other boys enough to be serious with them. He was always involved in and aware of what was going on in the group. When he did not like what was happening, he might hide behind other boys, or slouch against the wall, or lie down and pretend to sleep; but he was always taking in and analyzing. When he liked what was happening, Frank became radiant. He often remarked after the class that it had been "beautiful" or "magical."

This intelligent and sensitive boy learned a great deal about people in the course, and outgrew his initial fear of movement to become one of the most abandoned dancers.

Eighteen:
TURNING ON
WITHOUT DRUGS:
A HIGH SCHOOL CLASS

To get the students' view of an improvisational drama course, the members of one of George's classes were interviewed two days after the course was finished. These high school seniors—intelligent, articulate, and sensitive—were well equipped to analyze their improvisational drama experience. They were from privileged families and a prestigious high school, and their problems were different from those of the desperately deprived inner-city adolescents described previously. Many of them were drug-taking, directionless youths suffering from enormous confusion of values.

George taught the class as a staff member of the Training Teachers of Teachers program at the Harvard Graduate School of Education. The class met for three hours on Tuesday nights for thirteen weeks. Of the twenty-three students, twenty-one were enrolled in the course at their high school. They had selected improvisational drama from a variety of electives and received regular credit for it toward high school graduation. The other two students were high school dropouts who could not stand school; they took the course for pleasure and received no credit. No letter grades were given to any of the students, as grades are among the most efficient barriers between teachers and pupils.

The students were interviewed by Farnum Gray in small groups or singly. George was not present, so that they would be as open as possible in discussing the course. Although their school year had just ended, the students thought their group would be able to continue into the summer, as they had requested. As it turned out, they had already had their last meeting, but they did not know that, and they seemed to look forward to reaching new heights. The names of the students have been changed, but the dialogue included is accurate.

PICKING UP VIBRATIONS

Before his first class with the high school group, George had cause for apprehension. He had been informed that most of his students were involved in the drug culture of their comfortable suburban community. Kids who are involved in the drug scene frequently believe they are in an enlightened "free" state, in which they need only to "get into myself and do my own thing." George feared that the students would resent his authority and the physical activity imposed on them—that they would want only to sit down, rap, and pick up one another's "vibrations." He doubted that the course would be productive if he allowed the students to move as little and talk as much as they would if given a choice.

For the first class, George planned to have mostly nonverbal activity, since he had been told that kids in that community often hid behind great swirls of verbiage. The students took seats on the floor in a circle. George let them sit quietly for a moment, then stepped into the center and began to clap. There was no music, and he changed the beat frequently.

"Be with me," George said, and the students started to clap with him. Looking each student in the eye, and keeping the beat, George said, "Share this with me! Share it with others!" They turned to each other, keeping the beat. "Now, share it with somebody else." George moved about the room, and the students got up and began moving about, sharing the beat with different people. "Share it with someone in this room whom you don't know very well."

By the end of that first exercise, the kids were taking the class seriously. They knew it would not be the same old thing. By simply clapping and sharing it with other people—without the verbalization they had come to rely on—they had felt an involvement with each other and with George.

A couple of the students came to that first class high on drugs. George said nothing then, but at the start of the second class he told the students, "I want us to turn on without dope. Besides, it's not fair for some people to come to class stoned and others not." He established a flat rule against the use of drugs before or during class.

Some of the students used drugs heavily. Most of them smoked grass, many had dropped acid, and a few were using heroin. Getting kids to quit drugs was not part of the purpose of the course, and we don't know that the course helped any of the kids get off drugs.

However, their serious discussions helped them to understand their motives for drug taking. They were generally agreed that they used drugs to gain prestige and to conform to the crowd. Many of them learned how to turn on without drugs, and one boy who had used heroin and virtually everything else said that he used drugs much less as the course progressed.

LEARNING A STRUCTURE OF MOVEMENT

As George got to know the kids, he found them drifting and unstructured. They tended to fantasize a lot and to see their lives as morbid tragedies. When they came to class feeling depressed and introspective, George had to decide whether to go along with them. When the fourth class dragged, George let it go. But when the next class also started off slowly, George said, "You were down for the last class, and you're down today. What's wrong?" The students hastened to tell him their problems, and how depressed they were. George told them that if they wanted the class to be interesting and vital, they would have to take the responsibility of working at it. But the choice was theirs: if they wanted another unexciting class, they could keep on dragging.

The students knew they could have upbeat, exciting classes because they had done so before. Because George was able to point out why the class was up or down on different days, and because he showed them how they could repeat their peak experiences, they wanted to learn the procedures that he used. The study of procedures in the course interested them enough that they were willing to take responsibility for the progress of the class.

The students' need for structure, for ways of working together, showed itself in their desire to understand structural procedures. Through the volatile ups and downs of adolescence, they were always searching. Without encouragement to search outside themselves, they turned their desperate searching within and became more confused.

George's methods of getting people to work together fascinated most of the students. They wanted to learn the techniques that George was demonstrating in class. They admired George's leadership tactics so much that most tried to emulate him when they got their chance to lead the class. They were invariably disappointed that they could not control the class as well as George did.

"George leads people. He drives people," Wayne said. "He can do that because he probably doesn't care much about the opinion of the class towards him as long as they are obeying. I couldn't get away with it."

"Are you ever offended by George's way of handling the class?" Farnum asked.

"No! No! I think it's fine. I tried it myself; couldn't do it. I just think it's so great, 'cause it works so well."

Many junior high school students (and a few teachers) have gone through courses or workshops without ever realizing that George was exercising authority over them. These high school kids, though, were well aware that their class was firmly structured.

Wayne and some of the other students felt confused when they discovered that, although they had thought they would rebel against any authority, they had no desire to rebel against George. After discussing this paradox with George, the students decided "He has authority, and the only way to end his authority would be through revolution. The only effective revolution would be to just remove him from the class." The students decided that since they had no objection to George's authority, and in fact liked the class the way he ran it, they would not revolt. Some seemed surprised to discover that revolution is a choice rather than an obligation.

ENCOURAGING OBJECTIVITY

Although teaching these intelligent and articulate youngsters was an exciting task, it would have been easy for George to let the students get bogged down in rap sessions and in psyching each other out. They would have loved to make the course a sensitivity group, and George continually had to direct them toward more objective discussion of their experiences. In the interviews after the course, some of the students recalled an improvisation that had helped them realize the benefits of objectivity in observation and discussion.

In this improvisation, George put Barbara and Helen on the stage and told them to form a relationship without speaking. Barbara turned her back on Helen, rejecting her with a pout, as Helen persistently tried to be friendly. In the discussion afterwards, the students probed quite imaginatively into the two girls' minds. They said that Helen had tried to pull Barbara out of her shell. Barbara was suffering terribly and wanted to come out of her shell, but she could not. Her suffering was so great that she had to withdraw and be alone, defending herself from the world's cruelty.

"Let's look at what they're doing physically, not speculate about their feelings," George said. To the annoyance of some of the students, George insisted that they focus their attention on the girls' physical actions: Helen tried to be friendly with Barbara, who repeatedly rejected her.

"Who was in control?" George asked. Now the students, having a clear idea of what had happened physically, were able to see that Barbara was in control. Her motivation was not apparent, but the students knew that she was in control, and they were able to discuss the incident without projection or distortion.

A DISTURBING BREAKTHROUGH

A round-faced girl named Phyllis quickly became unpopular with most of the students, although she seemed unaware of it. She had a number of unengaging traits, but the worst was her bubbly obsequiousness, which was continually exhibited in remarks like, "Oh, this is the most wonderful class I've ever had! And George is just a perfect teacher!"

"I just looked at her sometimes and I really felt like turning round and puking," Terry recalled. "She'd just say these things like, 'Wow! The ocean's so wet!'" Nevertheless, Terry said, "It got so I felt sorry for her, because she was sort of a scapegoat or something."

"She has this insincere manner," Wayne said. "Totally empty!"

In one class, George overheard Wayne hissing that he wished Phyllis would shut the hell up. "Why don't you say something to her?" George asked Wayne. "Nah, I couldn't," Wayne replied.

The following week, George put Phyllis and Wayne on the stage and said, "Do what you like." Wayne lay on the floor with his feet toward Phyllis and ignored her. Pieces of confetti were left on the floor from a previous improvisation, and Phyllis occupied herself by throwing confetti at Wayne. One of his feet had been injured not long before, and Phyllis tapped the sore foot several times. Neither spoke until George reminded them, "You may talk."

Wayne said, "Phyllis."

"What?" Phyllis said.

"Nobody in the class likes you," Wayne informed her.

The group had been avoiding difficult situations such as this one. Cliques and personal dislikes were holding back the group's progress, but nobody mentioned these problems openly. Because the group met only once a week, it seemed discouragingly unlikely that they would make a breakthrough in their relationships unless George asserted himself somewhat more than usual.

Typically, the discussion began with the students trying to smooth things over. They decided Wayne had exploded that way only because Phyllis had tapped his sore foot—without knowing it was sore, of course.

Then George asserted himself. "It appeared to me that there was hostility on the stage right from the first." The students asked what evidence of hostility George had seen. He asked, "When Phyllis is throwing things at Wayne, and he is rejecting her by conspicuously ignoring her, could it be that there is hostility?" Finally the students began, somewhat hesitantly, to discuss the hostility.

"I apologized but I said I was still glad I did it," Wayne said later. "And what *she* was worried about was she never thought about anybody disliking her. . . . I didn't understand that at all. In class, we would sit there and snicker and point directly at her and she would sit there with that smile. She said she didn't know feelings were that intense and she affected people in that way. I said a lot of people in the class felt the same way as I did. . . . It was obvious after they started talking. It was super-tense in the class. It was the first time everybody stopped being a nice guy."

It also was the first time in the class that Phyllis lost her buoyancy. When Wayne repeated that he thought no one in the class liked her, and a couple of the other boys joined in, she burst into tears and ran to the bathroom. When she returned from the bathroom, it was to announce that she could never face the group again: she would have to drop the course. "I felt so ashamed!" Wayne recalled. "I thought, 'Wayne, you louse!' "

George asked the group, "Are we here to change things? Or are we going to feel guilty if we disturb relationships that are well established but are false and destructive? Are we here to make discoveries? Or are we to feel so guilty about what we think or feel that we will try not to discover anything that makes us uncomfortable?"

The students seemed to understand what George was saying. Phyllis acknowledged that she had been throwing a temper tantrum and said she would keep coming to the course after all. Some of her classmates told her that they respected her courage.

After that, the group opened up markedly. Discussion became much more free on a personal level, and the group lost much of the cliquishness that had impeded its progress. The feelings about Phyllis had been so intense, and the scapegoating of her so pervasive, that no honest examination of relationships between people in the class could have been made as long as the feelings about her were concealed. When these feelings were brought into the open, many of the students were led to think of alternative ways of dealing with situations involving people they did not like.

At the end of the semester, Phyllis told Farnum the course had been just great. A bit wistfully, she added that she thought classes were best when they were fun all the way through. "I've loved to act—just loved it—ever since I can remember. We should stick to acting and other fun things and not get into other things," she said.

When Wayne was asked what he had learned from the experience, he said, "Well, I think, now I would take her aside and say, 'Look, what you're doing is annoying me.' I don't think I'd say, 'I don't like you,' 'cause that's pretty crushing. If you liked somebody, and they said they don't like you, then that's a big drag. And I don't think I'd ever do that again. But, it made me think a little more honestly about how I do things. About how I act with people."

THE STUDENTS ARE FORCED TO TAKE OVER

In the usual sequence of group development, the first stage is one in which the members rely heavily on the leader. In the second stage, the group wants to rebel against the leader. With this particular group, the second, or counterdependent, stage did not develop. The students continued to rely on George.

When George suggested that the time had come for them to take over the class, they asked him, "Are we ready to take this class over, or not?" George said, "Well, are you?" The students wanted George to tell them what to do, but he thought it important for them to have responsibility, and halfway through the course he started assigning pairs of students to run each class. It later became evident that he should have continued running the class himself for a while longer. In a group interview after the course ended, Peggy said, "The only criticism I have of the course is that I don't think that we were really equipped to run classes when George had us start doing it. I didn't really feel ready. I think that if we'd been meeting more times a week, or if we'd been meeting for a longer period of time, it would have been easier."

Betty commented, "We'd have gotten to a higher plateau if George had run it. I mean, if we'd had the class twice a week, and he had run it once a week and let the kids run it the other time, that would have been great."

Asked for his criticism of the course, Ernst said, "Only that I think George had it in his mind that what he wanted to work up to was having kids run the class. I don't think we were ready to. I guess he thought since we only had five classes left we'd better be doing that, and I don't think people were ready to. That's the only thing I could criticize. . . . When Sarah and I did the warm-ups, . . . all the people were just fucking around and making a lot of noise and I got really angry, . . . I thought, well, they weren't going to listen to me. I really prepared myself. That was sort of a safety device, . . . thinking it wasn't going to work anyway. . . . and you could see that if George had done the exact same things everybody would have been nice and thought about it and been real serious. They won't respect you because you're not older than them or something. . . ."

GIVING CONCRETE HELP

Peggy and Betty recalled an exercise Ernst had created, in which half the class had formed a circle facing outward. The other half formed a circle around the first circle, with each person in the outer circle facing a person in the inner circle. Then Ernst said, "Hug each other." That accomplished, everyone in the outer circle moved one person to the right and the hugging was repeated. The circle continued all the way around amidst embarrassed giggling.

At the end of the class, George pointed out to the students that one of their problems in leading the class was that they did not give sufficient concrete help. "You cannot just tell people to look at each other and then hug, because our society has made us very self-conscious about that," he said.

George then instructed the class to get into two concentric circles again, and to close their eyes. They stood there for two minutes, with the room quiet except for the sound of breathing. "As you stand there, relax your body," George said. "Feel the blood coursing through your blood vessels. Concentrate on that. I want you to think of a very happy day. Was it a spring day? See that day. What was it like? What was the sky like? What did it smell like? What did it feel like? What was it that made you happy that day? Trace the events. Think about what happened and feel that happiness within you."

He put on some light, airy classical music. Most of the kids, standing there with their eyes closed, were euphoric. George picked out those who did not look serene. Standing directly in front of each in turn, he gave individual encouragement to those who seemed to be having trouble feeling happiness. Then, "Open your eyes, Look at the person opposite you. Hug that person." George used the word *hug* because he wanted the kids to know that he was giving the same basic assignment that Ernst had given them. "Hug that person, and make him feel that feeling from within you. Share it with him. Keep hugging. Share that feeling."

Betty said that George "added a dimension" to the experience. The dimension he added amounted to helping the students concentrate on an emotional experience and then communicate it to other people. The activity became a communicative experience instead of a mechanical expression of the love one "ought" to feel.

From this experience, the students got the idea that just telling someone to think deep thoughts or have beautiful feelings isn't enough; the communication of a specific experience is necessary. The kids understood it because it happened; they saw it and felt it. If George had sat down and talked with the students about making experience specific or giving concrete help, it would have meant little. But he helped them create things within themselves through physicality. The students understood the experience of tracing events and physical actions and of concentrating on the objective.

Wayne discussed this point in his interview. "You couldn't teach improvisational drama . . . like a lecture. You have to teach it very emotionally." He demonstrated how one of his teachers stands in front of his class with his jaw set. "A person who looks like that could not really teach anything," Wayne grumbled.

AN EMBARRASSING ASSIGNMENT

Betty and Wayne were interviewed separately. Yet when asked to describe a class that stood out in their minds, they both unhesitatingly blurted out the same story. Wayne had been in charge of the class. In making his plans, he wanted to deal with the fact that the students were "horny" and acted very silly about sex. He thought that if he gave them some rather shocking assignments having to do with sex, the students would have to deal with the assignments seriously and would learn to be more mature in discussing sexual matters.

Wayne started by putting Betty and Barry on stage. He told them that he was going to give them a prop and that they were to use it in an improvisation. Then he tossed Betty a condom.

"First, I got hysterical," Betty recalled. "Then I started yelling at him, saying that I didn't think it was very nice that he made me buy it, and that asking the pharmacist for it was the most embarrassing thing I'd ever done in my life. Afterwards, they complimented me," Betty said, almost choking with laughter. "They said I was very *real.*"

It had been more embarrassing for Wayne than for Betty. He cringed at the recollection. "Everyone went nuts. I . . . thought, 'Uh, oh! Cut the improv!' It wasn't working out. . . . It just made me steer clear of the subject for the rest of the class. . . . You have a lot of things to think about in running a class; you gotta keep the people together. . . . They have to accept the ideas of the person who's telling them what to do. They have to accept those ideas as legitimate ideas. And if you lose their respect, . . . they don't listen to you anymore."

IS THE TEACHER THE WHOLE THING?

One of the questions we are asked most frequently is, "Could anyone but George teach this?" Of course, other people can, and do. But we hear the question so much that Farnum asked it of five members of the class. "Do you think the course you've just taken was successful only because George taught it? Was it George and your relationship with him that made the course go, or could it have succeeded with another teacher?"

"Oh, yes!" Peggy said, "I didn't have the kind of relationship with George that Bob and some of the other kids had. I really think of George as just the guy who leads the thing. And I got just as much, you know, it was *my* course, even though I didn't strike up a close relationship with George."

Betty agreed. "But that's not what makes it. The fact that he knows how to run it; that he's smooth, and the way he knows how to get you to do it." Once again, the students showed their fascination with George's methods of getting people to work together. "Even when he makes mistakes, you just know he's thinking," Peggy said.

Farnum asked Wayne, "Suppose that course were being taught by someone who didn't have the grace of movement or the colorful appeal that George has, but who knew the techniques and knew how to teach it. Do you think it would still be a good course?"

"I think it *would* be a good course," Wayne replied. "I think you've got to have a firm person. [But] it would have to be a human being to teach that class because it's a human beings' class."

HITTING A PLATEAU

Farnum asked of one group, "Did you at any time have hopes for the class that were not met?"

"Yeah," Bob said, "the thing I really hoped for was complete unity for this class. We were not really together as much as I'd hoped we would be. I wanted everybody to be such a close, intimate group. . . ."

"There wasn't the time, you know, we were only meeting once a week," Peggy said. Betty agreed. "After the first three meetings, it seemed like we were going like this." With her hand, she traced a steeply rising diagonal line. "And then we kind of went like this." She showed the line leveling out to a gentle rise. "We kept on going there; we didn't keep on going up. It would have been good if we had. We *could* have if we'd had two or three meetings a week." The others also attributed this leveling off to the students' taking over the course too early or to having only one session a week.

Farnum continued, "What were you getting up to that you hoped would continue growing?"

"Just a group feeling. I can't think of any better word than that. Just a feeling between the kids," Sarah responded, and the others nodded vigorously.

WHAT DID THEY GET OUT OF IT?

"I've gotten to know people that I never would have bothered to get to know," Peggy said, "and I've gotten to like people that I probably would never have liked. . . . Everybody is feeling inhibited together, and when people start feeling uninhibited, opening themselves up and feeling a little vulnerable . . . you just get to know them. I give them more of a chance, I suppose, in that situation, because I know how inhibited I was in that situation. Just from that experience I find myself not judging people as quickly. You also see another side of people you don't normally see."

Terry recalled how he had learned something about his own anger through an argument with Marvin. "I said some things about his personality, I think. I got angry. It was one of the few times in the last few years that I've gotten angry. I called him an asshole. Usually after I get angry I just puff up and go away thinking I did the right thing. But this time I stopped and thought, 'Why am I getting angry?' And the whole class helped me and said, 'What are you doing?' "

"Were you expecting, when you started the course, to learn something like that?" Farnum asked.

"No," Terry said thoughtfully, "I was expecting a lot of learning how to act, learning how to project your voice, learning give-and-take with other people. Looking back on it, that happened as much as I thought it would happen, but the taming down of inhibitions and the gaining of freedom has been so much more intense than I expected. . . ."

Wayne volunteered, "When I used to do improvs, I thought the only way I could do an improv was to be funny. . . . But I can get up there now and—without embarrassment—do a serious piece.

"And I've started doing my own thinking again, which is something I haven't done for a long time. Even when I couldn't feel any cosmic energy, I still was having my own thoughts. And I feel free to express them."

All students were strongly positive about the course, and all described having undergone such changes as lessening of inhibitions. Terry, beaming with pride, described a positive change in himself that was somewhat unexpected. He had become less tolerant of the "hypocritical stuff" required of him at school. This showed in his grades, which had dropped sharply.

Students said their attendance was far better in improvisational drama than in their other courses, though we did not check records to verify this. Bob, who had perfect attendance in drama, said he did not attend a single class in any other course from Christmas through May.

Some of the boys said that the course had inspired them to write, and George met with them occasionally to discuss their work. Terry, in particular wrote some sparkling essays.

It seems that most people who go through a powerful group experience tend to believe that they—and probably everyone else in the group—have undergone a transformation. No matter how much people are warned that change is difficult, takes a long time and much effort, and is subject to almost certain relapses, they think that everything will be different henceforth. In this class, as with others, the inevitable disillusionments came hard. But the general feeling about the class was very positive.

Nineteen:
SOME
RESEARCH FINDINGS

A high school class similar to the one described in the preceding chapter was the subject of extensive research into the effects of improvisational· drama on students. The varied research techniques used all tended to corroborate each other. A definite trend to positive development was indicated, although the sampling was too small for the results to be statistically significant.

George taught this course and carried out the research as part of his doctoral work at the Harvard Graduate School of Education. The class met twice a week for a total of twenty-eight meetings.

For research to have been conducted without being part of the learning process for students and teachers seemed contrary to the open, honest climate that was desirable for the class. So the research design included the students as active participants in gathering data and as major sources of information about their own personal development.

Six major research techniques were used:

1. Administration before and after the course of the Loevinger Sentence Completion Test, which locates the subject's stage of ego development. Expert analysis of pre- and postcourse results determined trends and extent of development, and these results were compared with those of a control group.

2. Analysis by independent observers of videotapes of classes held early and late in the course to assess progress in the four areas of emphasis of the course: physical freeing, concentration, believability, and relationships.

3. A journal kept by George.

4. A record of observations kept by a nonparticipating peer of the students in the class.

Table 19-1. Some milestones of ego development[1]

Stage	Code	Impulse Control, Character Development	Interpersonal Style	Conscious Preoccupations	Cognitive Style
Presocial Symbiotic	I-1		Autistic Symbiotic	Self versus non-self	
Impulsive	I-2	Impulsive, fear of retaliation	Receiving, dependent, exploitive	Bodily feelings, especially sexual and aggressive	Stereotype, conceptual confusion
Self-protective	△	Fear of being caught, externalizing blame, opportunistic	Wary, manipulative, exploitive	Self-protection, wishes, things, advantage, control	
Conformist	I-3	Conformity to external rules, shame, guilt for breaking rules	Belonging, helping, superficial niceness	Appearance, social acceptability, banal feelings, behavior	Conceptual simplicity, stereotypes, cliches
Conscientious	I-4	Self-evaluated standards, self-criticism, guilt for consequences, long-term goals and ideals	Intensive, responsible, mutual, concern for communication	Differentiated feelings, motives for behavior, self-respect, achievements, traits, expression	Conceptual complexity, idea of patterning

Autonomous	I-5	Add:* Coping with conflicting inner needs, toleration	Add: Respect for autonomy	Vividly conveyed feelings, integration of physiological and psychological, psychological causation of behavior, development, role conception, self-fulfillment self in social context	Increased conceptual complexity, complex patterns, toleration for ambiguity, broad scope, objectivity
Integrated	I-6	Add: Reconciling inner conflicts, renunciation of unattainable	Add: Cherishing of individuality	Add: Identity	

*Add means in addition to the description applying to the previous level.

5. Journals kept by students in the class.

6. Independent interviews of students after the conclusion of the course.

The model of developmental stages used in this research was developed by Jane Loevinger. Loevinger recognizes eight stages, or milestones, of ego development. Table 19-1 summarizes the character traits, interpersonal style, conscious preoccupations, and cognitive style accompanying each stage of ego development. Movement from a lesser to a greater stage indicates positive development.

George's purpose in this class was to try to facilitate personal growth in the students, on the theory that exercising their capacities through improvisational drama helps students to move toward higher stages in the development of their egos.

THE LOEVINGER SENTENCE COMPLETION TEST

The Loevinger Sentence Completion Test was administered at the beginning and the end of the course to measure the personal growth and ego-development of the students. All results were shared with the subjects. Tests were scored and interpreted by Dr. M. C. Dowell of the Harvard Graduate School of Education. The scores were converted into a ten point scale, with a number assigned to each stage and to combinations of adjoining stages. For example, stage I-3 (conformist) is number 4 on the scale. Stage I-4 (conscientious) is number 6. A subject falling between stages I-3 and I-4, having some of the characteristics of each stage, would receive a score of 5.

*Loevinger Stages**		*Scaled Score*
I-2	Impulsive	1
Delta	Self-protective	2
Delta 3		3
I-3	Conformist	4
I-3/4		5
I-4	Conscientious	6
I-4/5		7
I-5	Autonomous	8
I-5/6		9
I-6	Integrated	10

*Loevinger Stage I-1 was not included because a person in the presocial or symbiotic stage of ego development could not be a student.

Complete results for both pre-test and post-test administrations were available for eleven students. Using a correlated t-test, the change in scaled scores between pre- and post-tests was not statistically significant, partly because of the small sample size. The class was rated at a scaled score of 4 on the pre-test. This is equal to the I-3, or conformist, stage in the Loevinger system. Conventional roles and social virtues are parroted and idealized, authority is accepted without question, and rules must be followed. The subject often thinks and talks in cliches. On the post-test scores, the class average was 4.4. Although this difference is not statistically significant, the direction of the shift is toward the I-3/4 stage of the Loevinger scale. This stage is marked by the beginning of an "inner life" and more concern for interpersonal relations. Thought patterns are more abstract and differentiated. Human behavior is no longer seen as random, and there is a beginning of concern for "process."

While we cannot be certain that this growth resulted from the improvisational drama course, test results for the control groups—standard psychology classes—showed regression in ego development between the beginning and end of the course.

VIDEOTAPING

Two classes were videotaped, one at the beginning of the course and one toward the end. The tapes were evaluated by two independent viewers, Dr. David Tiedeman and Miss Victoria Draper. Dr. Tiedeman is a professor at the Harvard Graduate School of Education, and has a good understanding of the principles of improvisational drama.

The evaluators were not told which videotape represented which class, so that they would not be influenced in their judgment of progress. Both evaluators were instructed to evaluate the students on the four basic aspects of the course: physical freeing, concentration, believability, and relationships. They were also asked to evaluate George's handling of the classes.

Since both evaluators had extensive knowledge of improvisational drama, it was hoped that an open-ended evaluative procedure would be least prejudicial to their findings. They were not requested to look for particular improvements or to seek out failings; form and procedure were left up to the evaluators. Since the evaluations corroborate each other, only one is included here.

Summary of Tape 1

A group of about twenty high school students were led by the instructor in a series of exercises lasting about forty minutes. The students seemed to follow the teacher and looked to him or others in the class for instructions. Their movements were hesitant, as if they were unaccustomed to paying attention to their own actions or those of their classmates. In one exercise, "make the shape of a tree," several girls shaped their arms and the other students seemed to mimic their position. In free dancing, most movements were jerky and not composed; a student would stop in the middle of one routine, pause, and then think of an opposite move. Tremendous vitality was shown in free movement exercise, although the group tended to "collapse" when given a specific imitation or when asked to stop, huddle on the floor, and wait for the next instruction. The class kept a paced, orderly routine, but there was little sign of self-enforced concentration between sets. Several students declined to participate in the animal movement exercise.

The assignments began with the most general, least personalized movements. The class progressed in the following sequence:

1. Think of an animal and portray it—all together.
2. Use animal movements and be a person—all together.
3. What kind of animal are you? Act it—all together.
4. Student is handed a slip of paper with the name of another person in the class. Act the animal image of that person—done singly.

As the class moved from assignment two to three, some of the students became more believable. But when they were asked by the teacher to portray another person in the class, many became jerky in their movements, or stopped entirely, probably because of both inhibition and lack of concentration. Some animals that had negative connotations, such as the snake, ape, and squirrel, seemed to embarrass the actors.

Summary of Tape 2

The second tape of the same class was made toward the end of the semester. The first exercises were done blindfolded. The students moved randomly, patting one another's heads. Then a recording of

African music was put on and they danced with uninhibited movement and sense of rhythm. They didn't seem unsure of themselves
and the hazards of dancing in a group of unseen flailing arms and
legs; instead they laughed as they bumped and touched and seemed
free. One of the girls was the group leader for the entire session and
the teacher was out of view the whole time.

After warm-ups, the leader asked the class to act as though they
were moving through jello, then through cotton candy. They showed
good variety of movement. When asked to dance in couples with
hands touching and "discover your partner," they touched each
other's bodies without embarrassment whether they were boy-girl,
girl-girl or boy-boy. After body exploration they returned to the
faces of the other person, as if the identity of the person were more
in the face than in bodily shape. Even though they were blindfolded,
students seemed to trust their partners. Even the exercise of crouch-
ing on the floor and trying to reach out and hit each other produced
giggles, not cringes.

Next, three students, two girls and a boy, sat blindfolded on the
floor and cooked dinner. The audience was entertained as they
bumped into each other, forgot where the potatoes were, or couldn't
find the cake pans. In the discussion of the exercise, they were asked
whether the blindfolds bothered them, and they replied that they
had gotten used to them very quickly. One boy in the class observed
that one of the girls had gotten pushed out of the action while the
other girl assumed leadership in inventing cooking tasks and trying to
figure out where people were. Aside from the question of leadership,
which was not analyzed at length (no psychological imputations
from the audience), the audience focused on the fact that the group
forgot things or misplaced them.

The next set of tasks was to sell Kippo, an imaginary product, first
without words, then in an imaginary language, then in English. All
three improvisations were successful, laughed at, and applauded. One
girl, who was assigned the third problem, declined to participate. In
this class, people were allowed to drop out of activities, and there
was no pressure on them to overcome shyness or to perform.

Verbalization did not seem to be a complete hindrance to movement, although sometimes the entertaining aspects overshadowed the
actors' sense of movement, perhaps because it is hard to focus on
both at once. One positive change from the first tape was that all
group members were engrossed, and they all played along when they

had a chance. When handed an imaginary marijuana cigarette, with the admonition, "I must warn you it's illegal," they got into the action. Some put up resistance to the saleswoman—"I might get arrested,"—but most enacted a marijuana high convincingly. When asked to comment, the group declined. The group didn't try to give overly elaborate interpretations to movement or speech—only when they didn't understand something did they express concern for the meaning.

The next two situations were similar to each other. One student was withdrawn and attempted to get the other person involved in her problem. In the first skit, the actors couldn't get going and it fizzled. The second skit was more successful, but still the audience became frustrated. The discussion was cut off by the end of the tape so it was hard to tell whether or not the class had concluded anything from the exercise. It seemed difficult for the boy to avoid the girl under the terms of the role when his personal empathy urged him to try to understand her. This is an example of the tension that can be produced when an acted situation clashes with the feelings of the actor. Perhaps this helps the actors to understand the ambiguity of their own feelings when another person asks them for help and yet they must maintain their own autonomy.

Comparisons of the Two Tapes

Comparison of the two tapes shows great development of the class in three areas: autonomy/leadership, control of movement, and imagination of character. By the time of the second taping, they were more able to work together in verbal situations, they were closer together in their concern about bringing off a group situation, and they showed more enjoyment in their spontaneous successes and goofs. I saw little of the self-consciousness that was apparent in the first tape. I was also pleasantly surprised to find that the class, although more polished, remained simple in its activities and avoided two characteristics I would have guessed would emerge: overanalysis of situations and overacting. The teacher wisely stayed out of the action completely, even when a situation stalled and he could have intervened. It seemed worthwhile for the class to experience its own frustrations, both as viewers and as doers, and to help each other regain momentum.

I tried to look at the two tapes (it soon became clear which one was made early in the semester and which one toward the end) and think of what effect the course had on the students in terms of the changes noted above. Part of the growth of the class was due to the closeness of the students over a period of months. But beyond that, I think they were exposed to a variety of unique situations and could see how they were different from, and similar to, the rest of the class. This respect for individual differences, if carried over into their relationships with others, could bring new appreciation for the complexities of other people. And focusing on tasks emphasizing physical movement and the senses helped relieve anxiety about exposing themselves psychologically at a time in their lives when their own relationships may be very undecided. There seemed to be none of the cliques that I had expected, and all seemed to take responsibility for the momentum of the class.

Conclusion

Both evaluators noted that there seemed to be less self-consciousness and inhibition of physical movement in the second tape than in the first. Also, concentration which produced more "controlled and natural" improvisational acting was manifested in the second tape. This "natural" quality tends to corroborate the impression that the students had become more "believable" in their acting. Finally, both evaluators noted improvement in the relationships aspect of the course on the second tape. The fact that the students handled the later class without the teacher's assistance and seemed to be interested in helping the student-leaders suggested increased ability in relationships.

The evaluators stressed that the students seemed to be learning about their own individuality. The variety of original responses to the situations to which the students were exposed allowed them to explore their own behavior and the behavior of others in the group.

TEACHER'S JOURNAL

In his journal, George recorded observations, descriptions, and analyses of each class. In reviewing his notes, he found that the early lesson plans, concentrating on the four bases of improvisational drama, pressured the students to begin self-exploration even before they had freed themselves from physical inhibition. Almost every lesson plan had improvisations that, for the students, were implied questions: "Why am I moving this way?" or "What does this movement mean?"

His interpretations during the first third of the course centered around the questions, "How do I get these kids to explore their behavior?" and "Why aren't they exploring?" Clearly, cues from the students' behavior were telling him to stop pushing them into explorative processes and to allow them to decide for themselves when they should explore. He recognized the problem and realized that his desire to push the students was for his own purposes (including research for his thesis) and not for the students'. He wrote in his journal at that time:

> We had a rather difficult discussion today—there seems to be a degree of hostility directed toward me by several members of the group. I do feel, however, that hostility is justified. I have been pushing too hard—and have been worried that they would not learn—or experience sufficiently—would not start exploring their behavior. What a bag to get into! I have been focusing too much on my wants and needs and too little focused on others'.

Thesis considerations and his own need for success had to be pushed aside if the class were to work. In a talk with the class, George acknowledged his errors. The lesson plans and interpretations that followed showed a marked improvement.

Gradually, the students' fears of exposure disappeared. Intense discussion periods occurred frequently and naturally. Midway through the course it became evident that the students were now actively involved in exploring their expressive behavior, and George's interpretations showed clearly that he was listening to and watching the students more carefully.

NONPARTICIPATING OBSERVER

A student who had been a participant in a previous improvisational drama class at the school observed each class and kept a journal of his impressions, perceptions, thoughts, and feelings about the class, teacher, and students. The observer was present at every class and was advised that a daily analysis of what was occurring might be the best means of accomplishing his task. This was the only instruction he received.

Much of the content of his journal was irrelevant for research purposes. There were frequent nostalgic reminiscences of the previous spring's class. His journal did, however, describe the same developmental line suggested by the teacher's and students' journals.

In the early pages of his journal, the observer repeatedly noted people performing to gain peer approval.

Who are they performing for? From afar it all seems so graceful, still who are they performing for? Certainly not themselves. There is so much competition here, so much struggling to be noticed and appreciated by others that everyone appears to be running around in a circle. This group is so much a part of life. All life's problems, conflicts, frustrations are present in this group. But there is not enough self-esteem here.

During the third week, the observer wrote:

Things are much too intense. It looks like discussion is getting frank, but it isn't. People aren't opening—they're closing. There is too much hostility right now, and all the discussions are very defensive. Super, super conflicts. People talk and then other people cry to draw the attention away from the talkers. The vibes are bad. Things are tight. George should draw back for a bit and let things cool it.

By the fifth week, the observer noted that the class was beginning to emerge from the crisis period and to draw together as a group.

People have been directing their thoughts toward one another and not to George. They are coming together, a whole—people helping each other. What a change over two weeks ago! I warm just watching everyone. I wish I could describe what I see now better.

During the last week of the course the observer commented in his journal:

This group has shown that you only get out of a group what you're willing to contribute to it. Many doors have opened up for people in this group. Without this experience many people would not have grown as much as they did. They have learned to communicate with one another and are less afraid of revealing their feelings to each other. In a school where everyone wants to regiment the shit out of you, this course is a beauty.

Unfortunately, the observer's journal did not contain concrete description to illustrate his thoughts about the class. The main change noted by the observer is progression from competition for peer approval to a more open, communicative group. This would seem in harmony with changes noted by other assessment systems used in the research.

STUDENTS AS PARTICIPATING RESEARCHERS

The students kept personal records of their own learning and development. They were requested to write in their journals each day, about anything they wished. They were also asked to keep a section devoted to thoughts about improvisational drama: what they thought about the day's class, thoughts and feelings sparked by the course, or any concerns that came to light in the class.

The Loevinger Ego Development Model was used as the basis for analysis of trends revealed by the students' entries in their journals. Most of the students exhibited self-protective concerns (delta 3 in the Loevinger stages) in their initial journal entries.

I ask whoever picks up this journal by MISTAKE, please not to read what I have written. I don't want to share these thoughts. By asking people to write journals which he can read, George asks us to put a lot of trust in him. I wonder why we do it so willingly—why should we trust him? Will you see me as a person, or as a journal?

Another student expressed wishful thoughts that seemed both manipulative and self-protective:

I get the feeling that when teachers grade you it tells you if they like you. If you get an A the teacher really likes you. However, if I get anything below an A, I think I'm not liked at all. Whenever I take a test or write a paper I'm always thinking (What am I going to get—I have to get a good mark). I hate history class. I can't do the work. I hate Mr. H. because he hates me. I do poorly on every test even when I study for it. I can't wait until the drama class tomorrow because the people in the class are all so great and I think we'll all learn alot from one another, and I hope if I'm ever absent someone will notice. I was thinking about Brel again today and I wish I was there. . . . Forever.

This student's wish to be missed if she were absent from the drama class typified the self-protective behavior she manifested initially. Any criticisms of her actions in the class were met with sulking, childish retaliation. If rebuked or questioned by a peer, she would wait for an opportunity to exploit that person.

In the early sections of their journals several students showed themselves to be concerned with conformity. Although they seemed unaware of it, many of them tried very hard to conform to the behavioral standards set by more dominant persons in the group. Maureen, a bright senior who had participated in several encounter group sessions at the school, had announced her desire to love and care for each member of the group. Maureen set herself up as an experienced group participant, hoping to gain some degree of self-protective control in this manner. Her announcement had a strong effect on the group. Students who had not initially shown any particular interest in "group feeling" now became ostentatiously concerned for others. Tina wrote in her journal:

When Janet cried—I just hugged her—but didn't ask any questions. Carla came over while I was hugging Janet and said "What is it—are you upset about the class?" I felt far away from that—she seemed to be coming to conclusions and analyzing—she wasn't concerned—just prying and asking questions.

Carla had obviously been concerned, and her question seems gentle enough. But Tina, in her desire to gain peer approval for her "niceness" to Janet, rebuked Carla for trying to interrupt or share the limelight.

Later entries in these journals show more objective self-evaluation and a concern for communicating with peers, as these samples show.

I tend to judge people too harshly. When I am sad, I want people to help me. And yet when others are sad I don't always (usually don't) help them. I must learn to be more aware of other people's needs. Maybe this course will help me.

John wrote in his journal about the sixth week:

Underneath a person, underneath the words, the jokes, the aloofness, the self-assuredness is an area so vulnerable, so easily bruised and so beautiful. I saw some of it in Carla today, she was hurt, this inside thing was hurt and I wanted to tell her, to give her something.

Over the course of the semester people increased in respect for others and for themselves. Sally wrote in her journal during the eighth week:

I got upset in the class when people said that Eileen was being phony. Don't people realize that others might find them or me phony, too? If you respect people you don't call them phony, instead you try to understand them.

And Doris wrote:

I suppose all people want to be acknowledged by others. But I don't feel obligated any more to get people to know me. Like, I just want to let it happen.

I'm pretty selfish/self-centered at times because I feel that everything I do is for me—everything I want to happen is for me—and I don't consider other people. I think that's unappreciative but it's something I can change.

On the whole, the students' journals proved to be of greater value in developing improvisations for the class than in measuring ego development. There was so much personal material—writing devoted to experience about which we had little or no knowledge—that it was difficult to assess these journals. The students did, however, state almost unanimously that they enjoyed writing their journals and learned from them. Writing down their thoughts seemed to help the students objectify their experiences.

INTERVIEWS

At the end of the semester, each student was interviewed by an educator who had no previous connection with the class. The interviews were open-ended to allow students to discuss whatever seemed important to them. To facilitate this free expression, the interviewer began with one question and then probed further whenever the students touched on material pertinent to the research.

The research questions to be investigated were: What are the concerns of adolescents, and how has this course helped its students explore those concerns? The interviews were recorded and transcribed, and the interviewers offered comments about student behavior during the interview period that they felt might clarify the material presented. The initial question was: How has this course affected you?

Carla: To put it in twenty-five words or less. . . . It's been a really big learning experience. I've learned a lot about others and myself. It's been helpful in dealing with certain kinds of feelings. I'm also interested in theater, and it's helped me. I wish I could put it down more as practical applications outside of class or outside of drama. . . . But I've learned a lot.

I've met lots of people on a different plane than I would have known . . . before. Some I started out to hate, now I like. Some I started out to like, now I—It's been good relationships with people.

Interviewer: Could you be more specific about what you've learned?

Carla: Oh, I'm a very manipulative person. I've become more aware of my manipulations, of my making decisions for others, and of getting into their heads.

I learned to act—I'm a big attention person—I need a lot of attention. Now I'm more aware of that and I can control it or use it.

I learned that people have many of the same feelings like trying to get a friend to support you in a group when you feel alone. Many people do that.

I've learned about creative and new ways of teaching. I'm interested in teaching and I'll teach this summer. I will use it; it will apply to almost anything . . . and I'll use it.

Not to categorize it. It's not drama or psychology. It's a people experience. I don't know if this is good or bad, but I tend to make value judgments. The class has taught me to judge less and to get into other people's heads and to understand them, to find out that [judging] gets in the way of education. The good thing to say becomes the only thing to say.

In theory I've always known these things, but now I feel it. There is a big gap between what I am emotionally and intellectually. The gap is lessening. . . .

It became a . . . big emotional letdown when someone didn't come who helped me or meant something to me as a person. If a boy—friend, not a heartthrob or anything—didn't come I'd take it personally and feel disappointed.

I put myself on the line more easily than others, than everyone else in the class. Some people can do that. But I wasn't always so honest about it. But I would make myself very vulnerable. So others would use me as an outlet for their feelings about me or about themselves. And that started to get a little hard.

The course has definitely helped me to become aware of these things. This is a big thing. It helped me become aware of them. It helped me by the way I'd respond to people, and to improvisation, and I was helped with talks with George and also from my journal.

Don talked about his opposition to the Vietnam War, and about his disillusionment with the possibility of affecting the course of United States' involvement. He had spent the year closely involved with a group of friends he had met in a theater arts course.

Don: [This class has been] one of the few . . . that have been worthwhile. . . . Even the course in theater didn't do too much for me. Well, this really taught me a lot and showed me a lot.

I know that since the class, I've faced my feelings more often. I think about them more. I would usually simply accept them and just go along. Now, I sort of think about them and try to figure them out—understand them. It sort of helps, knowing why I feel a certain way.

One thing the class has really done for me: I'm a very quiet person. I usually don't find much use or reason for words. I think I've changed a little bit. I know I talk and react to people a lot more than I ever did. I generally used to dislike talking with groups or with a bunch of people, but it's so easy just to sit after an activity and talk with these people—associate. It was also very hard for me to get to know people. But it's been so easy with this group of people.

I think I've matured because of it, because I can look at myself and sort of understand, maybe, the way I act and sort of realize why I do things. I really think the structure of the class was good, and, I mean looking back, seeing how each thing was built on to each other—led up to something.

Tom, who had dropped out of school for a while, came to the class even when he wasn't going to school.

Tom: He makes it more like it's not a class, and—he's not really a teacher. I'm referring to George. . . . He doesn't hold the god figure of a teacher. I really liked my experiences with the class. It gives me a chance to try to see if there is a way I can express myself through motion and through movement and I just like to move. In other classes, it's just headwork, but not physical.

It's helped me to talk to other people freer . . . and accept easier that other people will react differently to the same thing, the same situation. You know sometimes if someone reacts differently than myself, I just might wonder 'Why? How Come? How come you don't see it this way?' And now, just through the class, I can—if someone understands something differently, I just go, 'Oh, yeah, yeah.' I can accept that easily, and usually I want to find out why they feel that way.

Oh, yeah, as far as how to get myself to do improvisations, to use myself as something, and why I should do something physical first to get into my head, to concentrate—I've learned things like that. If George gives the course next year, I think I'd like to observe it just to see what next year's people do.

These and the other interviews corroborate the developing hypothesis that improvisational drama has helped these students learn more about themselves through the study of their expressive behavior. Some statements made by the students seem vague. Some might be attempts to please the teacher, perhaps to help his research. If so, that does indicate positive feelings for the teacher, since there were no grades or other reasons to fear the teacher's displeasure.

The students generally felt they had learned to see other people in more comprehensive and less judgmental ways. They also expressed the opinion that the physical involvement of the course helped them understand many of their own thoughts. And almost all the students made comments suggesting that they had begun to explore their actions and behavior.

Perhaps the most frequent observation the students made was that improvisational drama gave them an opportunity to explore their feelings. In a school setting where much of the curriculum stresses intellectualism and academic achievement, improvisational drama emerged, in the students' perceptions, as the first classroom experience to encourage exploration of personal feelings.

The evidence of the interviews indicates that the students enjoyed and benefitted from the course. Obviously, the testimony of satisfied clients is suspect. But the interviews were conducted by independent interviewers who gave the students minimal clues as to what they should say.

OVERVIEW OF COLLECTED DATA

The students' postcourse interviews and their journals clearly indicated that they believed that this course was worthwhile and improved their understanding of their own behavior and motivations. The students also agreed that they had gained in understanding of people's differing needs and experiences. Generally, the students reported that they had become more relaxed, less frightened, and less inhibited in their physical movement.

The teacher's journal, lesson plans, and interpretations of classes confirmed the students' belief that the course helped them in personal development. And George gained greatly from the experience himself.

The Loevinger Ego Development Tests showed a trend to personal development, although the sample was too small for the results to be statistically significant. In contrast, the control groups (psychology classes at the same school) showed regression from pre- to post-testing on this instrument.

Evaluation of videotapes of the class taken during the semester indicated changes in the students. Independent evaluators felt that the students (a) progressed in control and freedom of physical movement; (b) became less self-conscious and less self-centered; (c) developed more effective interpersonal relationships with their peers; and (d) exhibited stronger initiative in the handling of the class.

Though these evaluations were of isolated classes and, therefore, not comprehensive in scope, they reinforce other evidence that improvisational drama helps students explore their own behavior and learn more about themselves.

An unobtrusive measure of the effect of the course was that several of the students went on to teach improvisational drama at summer camps. They were excited about teaching this material to younger kids. They developed lesson plans and began to construct methods of teaching consistent with the literature on improvisational drama. In general, a person learns a great deal by teaching someone else, and we speculate that their growth continued, perhaps accelerated, when they taught others. The students in the program found the teaching of improvisational drama a natural extension of this course.

Other students did seem to be physically and expressively freer after the course. They had less of the painful self-consciousness of body image so typical of adolescents, and they made significant beginnings, at least, in expressing very personal material to their peers. To us, these seem important achievements for the students.

NOTES

1. Jane Loevinger, "The Meaning and Measurement of Ego Development," American Psychologist 21 (1966): 195-217.

Twenty:
PREPARING
TEACHERS

In using improvisational drama to prepare teachers, we put them through experiences like those we want kids to have. We want teachers to know what the experiences feel like, as well as knowing the theory and structuring methods.

If a teacher is to be a psychological educator, the development of his sensibilities and human qualities is important. Since students learn from the behavior of each of their teachers, all teachers, unavoidably, are psychological educators to some extent. One of the difficulties of beginning teachers is that their most recent models have been university teachers. Methods and attitudes picked up from those teachers are usually inappropriate in teaching children and teen-agers.

In our teacher training courses, teachers in academic fields from social studies to mathematics have gone through experiences much like those we structure for children. They have found a wide variety of ways to use what they learned. Some have gone on to teach full-fledged improvisational drama courses. Others have adapted the techniques for courses in creative writing or social science, or made minor use of some techniques in mathematics courses. Many have found that the openness and perceptiveness toward students they learned in the course pervades their teaching. We have been particularly gratified to note that some of our adult "alumni" have become more daring, independent, and willing to use their imaginations.

Picking up cues from students, preparing the environment, setting a mood, encouraging physical involvement: a good teacher works constantly on all of these. In our courses, teachers can concentrate on learning these things phenomenologically; they do not have to divide their attention by preparing content.

When we conduct workshops with teachers, we are often impressed with how little they have actually thought about structure or experienced alternative kinds of structure. Some people in education persist in talking about the unresolvable dichotomy between structure and freedom. An interesting demonstration of this viewpoint occurred in an afternoon workshop for teachers from a huge ghetto junior high school in Philadelphia. During the discussion, George mentioned *The Divided Self* by R. D. Laing.

A young, slender man with a beatific smile and a halo of soft brown hair said he had read it and loved it. Later, the same young teacher spoke up again. "I've only been a teacher for two weeks. But I wonder how you can do something like this in a public school. They require you to keep control of the kids," he said with obvious distaste.

"I should hope so," George replied. "You accomplish nothing by inviting kids into a room and telling them they can do anything they want to. We begin the class in a controlled way and maintain a structure throughout."

The young man could not keep a look of amazed disappointment from his face. He had seen George as a kindred free spirit, and now he was talking structure. The class, he said, had been "beautiful, free and groovy," but he had not noticed that it had a strong structure. That he thought the class too unstructured to be held in a public school indicated that he was not yet able to analyze teaching constructively.

A fiftyish vice-principal nodded approvingly as George pointed out how effectively the relaxation exercises had brought the class to a state of quiet concentration. He was pleased that George conceded the necessity for order. He might mentally have gone a step farther and realized that the relaxation exercises were more psychologically sound than the common siddown-and-shuddup approach to bringing order.

There are probably many schools that would not permit the teaching of improvisational drama, but their reasons do not include lack of structure—at least not legitimately.

THE IDEAL PROGRAM

Although we have never had the time or money to put our ideal teacher training program into effect, here is how we think the improvisational drama part of the program should go.

The trainees would meet for one hour a day, five days a week, for sixteen weeks. For the first twelve weeks, they would go through the usual improvisational drama experiences four days a week. On Fridays, they would discuss the structure of the class, their readings on the subject, and so on. Toward the end of the twelve weeks, they would take turns leading the group. This would be followed by a four-week session during which each trainee would teach improvisational drama to students of the age he plans to teach. Experienced teachers would observe as many of these classes as possible, and the trainees would observe one another's classes. Also, they would discuss, with each other and with their instructor, the classes they had taught and observed.

Teachers have to make do with whatever training they can get. And in our teacher training programs, we have had to make do with whatever working conditions we could arrange. We have tried to give the participants as much of the improvisational drama experience as possible, to help them experience it much as their students will. At the same time, we have tried to help them understand how the class was structured, what was happening, and why.

For example, the teacher might start the discussion of an improvisation by saying, "Since we're all teachers, I'm going to start this discussion with a question I would not normally ask kids: What was the structure that I gave to this improvisation, and what was the content that the actors brought to it?"

INTERNS' REFLECTIONS ON IMPROVISATIONAL DRAMA

In a group taught by George in Philadelphia, the focus was on the development of six teaching interns in advanced degree programs at graduate schools of education. A handful of experienced teachers and counselors were also taking the course. In addition to their work in improvisational drama, each intern also taught Advancement School boys throughout the semester and did other work required by his university.

For the first eight weeks of the course, during which the class met daily, George had three basic purposes:

1. To help the interns explore themselves and some of their anxieties and prejudices in preparation for teaching
2. To enable them to understand emotive education and classroom

structure better through the improvisational drama experience and occasional discussion classes

3. To aid them in developing their own styles and methods of teaching while working with an accomplished teacher

During the last part of the first eight weeks, some of the classes were taught by individual interns. Teaching their peers gave them an opportunity to get more articulate criticism from the students' viewpoint than they could normally expect to get from kids, and being students in classes taught by different teachers gave them some fresh ideas.

For the last six weeks of the course, the interns took turns teaching improvisational drama to a daily class of twelve Advancement School boys. Each intern discussed his plans with George, and George and the other interns watched each class. At the end of each week, the group got together and discussed the week's classes.

During one of the classes led by an intern, a boy began acting out disruptively on the sidelines. The intern glanced at him and then quickly looked away. For the rest of the class, the disruptive boy continued to disturb his classmates.

When the interns gathered for their weekly discussion, George asked the intern who had taught the class why he pretended to ignore the disruption.

"I saw it," he said, "but I didn't know what to do about it. So I thought it would be better to act as if I didn't know about it, rather than admit that I knew he was doing it but that I didn't know what to do."

George said that pretending not to notice a student's bid for attention can be as much a denial of a student's existence as having him stand outside the classroom (a very damning form of punishment). "When a student acts out, it is better to validate the experience—to make some kind of affirmation of his existence," George said.

The only way to know for sure what would stop the disruption would be to try something that worked. For a starter, the intern might have said, "We need your help." If that had not worked, he could have used stronger methods until something did work.

This intern, who was studying to be a social science teacher, had the intellect and character necessary for a superb teacher. He had some of the tightness often found in young people who have worked hard to excel academically, but he seemed to begin working that out in the course. He used improvisational drama techniques the following year while teaching social studies in a Boston public school.

In his journal, he wrote that the course he took from George was

probably the best single experience I've had as an intern trainee. It is better than just having a supervisor criticize teaching in front of a videotape, because in ID the intern can be student and teacher almost at the same time. And the ID format neutralizes the subject matter and most of the content issues that worry a teacher and interfere with concentration on the effects of interaction, environments, verbal and nonverbal cues, etc.

A cool-talking black man with considerable teaching experience—particularly in New York street academies—took the course as part of a master's degree program at Antioch-Putney Graduate School of Education. He was imaginative and charismatic, and his teaching stressed becoming free and seeking cosmic experiences. He sometimes burned incense in his classes.

He wrote, "ID was extremely valuable to my development. I was initially quite skeptical about the relevance of ID to my teaching. But the end of the semester found me among your most zealous converts. . . . I learned that teaching is all about *everything*—not just cognitive stuff."

A girl in the University of Pennsylvania's M.A.T. program, preparing to be a mathematics teacher, was obviously going to be an extraordinary teacher. The lessons she taught were imaginative and daring. She wrote in her journal,

The experience with improvisational drama is very appropriate to teacher training and should continue to be a substantial part of the intern program at P.A.S. [Pennsylvania Advancement School]. Participating in the class this past semester has contributed to my growth, first, on a very personal level, by forcing me to observe myself in several situations and to identify and sometimes reconcile feelings and attitudes stimulated in these situations. [Promoting such self-exploration might alone justify its inclusion in a program of teacher training.]

Observations of my efforts at teaching ID gave me a greater overall feel for how I came across in the classroom and pinpointed problems of general classroom behavior I must deal with before I can successfully handle problems specific to my subject area. . . . Evaluation and criticism from sessions within my department (the Perceptual Development, or mathematics, Department at the Advancement School) were often too closely related to specific presentation of specific ideas or Perceptual Development materials.

Third, the exchange of comments not related directly to my teaching was in general very enlightening and often suggested totally new ways of considering educational experience—such as distinguishing between content and structure; the fact that learning does not have to be a 100% pleasant experience all of the time; and so on.

To fully benefit, one must make a strong commitment to some very strenuous and demanding work.

Her opinion that improvisational drama was suitable for use in the training of mathematics teachers was contradicted by another mathematics student in the University of Pennsylvania's M.A.T. program. He was shy and pleasant, but he never became comfortable with improvisational drama. He was the only intern who declined to teach a class. He wrote,

> I have mixed feelings about ID. While I enjoyed taking part in the class, and I can see that the experience can expand one's knowledge of himself, I did not see that teaching the ID class was as much of an aid toward teaching as other methods.
>
> Many techniques that can be used in drama cannot be carried over into subject areas and vice versa; what is a good technique for a math teacher may not be for a social studies or English teacher, etc. I would have much preferred critical analysis of my teaching in my own subject area.

An energetic young black woman who taught science took the course as part of her master's degree program at Temple University. She had previous teaching experience in the Teacher's Corps. She wrote,

> I think there should have been more time spent in ID without the kids. We were beginning to loosen up when we were "hit" with the kids. I realize the limitations put on you by time, but perhaps this is something to consider in the future. The ID classes were helping me a great deal and forced me to look at some things which I wanted left alone. This was good for me. As a teacher-training device the class with kids and adults gave me some insights into the way one wants to be perceived and the ways that people perceive you. More specifically, the class helped me in pulling ideas off the top of my head.

A big, bushy-bearded, jovial former Guggenheim fellow took the course as part of his master's degree program at Harvard. He was majoring in social studies and had been fascinated with improvisational drama from the first. This intern group did not begin taking drama until their second semester at the Advancement School, but during his first semester he frequently observed a class of kids taught by George. Thus, his improvisational drama experience was in four phases: observer, student, teacher of his fellow interns, and teacher of kids. He wrote,

> I liked observing drama, as I did first semester. I felt that I began to learn a lot by observing, especially in the general sense that whole possibilities of what the classroom might be began to dance in my head. In terms of specific techniques of observing, I am sure I would have gotten much more out of my first semester had I talked over what I saw with someone.

This intern was almost always sweet and happy. It came as a surprise to some of his colleagues when, while teaching a Human

Development course to our urban, underachieving boys, he finally reached the point where their constant testing got to him and he exploded. On several occasions, his temper boiled over and he punished students rather harshly.

Yet, when he was a student in George's course, the big fellow at first seemed incapable of expressing anything other than sweetness and light. He finally made an important breakthrough in the class when he was able to express hostility.

"You're shits! You're all shits!" he shouted at his fellow students, his face frozen with rage. "And George, you're a shit, too!"

Afterwards, not sure whether he was relieved or scared, he said he thought he had gotten an important glimpse of an aspect of himself that he would have to learn more about to continue developing as a teacher.

I liked being a drama student, for I found those fifty minutes a time when I could concentrate totally on self-expression. I felt free, if not comfortable, to express what I felt, and I enjoyed trying. Both the structure and the actual people involved made me feel relatively at ease to try something difficult—what I deemed scary. The joy came partly from the release of expression, but also from the change of pace.

But part of the enjoyment perhaps came from the fact that, if one learned of flaws through drama, then drama's setting was also the best one around for working on those flaws. Drama isn't like one of those new automobile clinics, filled with scads of electronic equipment, which are to analyze a car completely, produce a list of its ills, and then eject it back onto the street to find its own dishonest repair shops. In drama I got the feeling that if I was willing to try to deal with a problem, then it would be dealt with. That put the responsibility on me, but I was pretty reassured by the humanness of the setting—the acceptance and so on.

This intern also felt that the main weaknesses of the course were that the interns were not students long enough to get a thorough understanding of the experience, and that "somehow we all should have been started on adapting what we were doing in drama a little more consistently to whatever courses we were teaching."

PSYCHOLOGY 253

Psychology 253, Improvisational Drama, a fall semester graduate course at the Harvard Graduate School of Education, met only once each week for three hours. George put a limit of fifteen on the class, but so many students signed up for it that he finally accepted nineteen. All but one were either high school teachers or graduate students of education; there was one law student. The only grades for the course were pass and fail; George made it clear from the start that everyone would pass, so there was no pressure to get a good grade.

All of the students said they liked the class and learned a lot from it. Some thought this was The Way for them to teach. Others thought that it was not the best way for them to work with kids, although they predicted that the course would have a valuable influence on their teaching.

One young woman in the class was quite successful in teaching an improvisational drama course at Newton High School, near Harvard. She wrote, "I've used almost all of the exercises we have done in our Harvard class, spacing them out over a few weeks, interspersing them with other theater exercises, not necessarily following the sequence of our classes."

She found that many of the students in this privileged, suburban group feared physical contact. For example, when small groups of students became moving machines, they were "involved—but very little physical contact. I had to direct them to make physical contact," by saying, "Each part of the machine is connected to some other part." The blind sculpture exercise also helped to break down the barriers.

CANNED SENSITIVITY

A problem we encounter frequently in conducting improvisational drama classes for adults is that many of them have been exposed to superficial—sometimes entrepreneurial—sensitivity training and have learned some dishonest gimmicks for feigning sensitivity. They are liable to trot out their gimmicks at any time, and, of course, part of the game is that anyone who does not conform is condemned as insensitive.

The problem does not arise with teen-agers who have not been trained to be "sensitive," or with people whose work in effective groups actually has brought them to an advanced state of psychological understanding.

An ambitious young educationist in one of our classes pursued sensitivity as diligently as he did success, and for much the same reasons. He had read the books, and, needing something titillating to talk about at a weekend group, he imagined himself in love with a woman other than his wife. He sometimes told other educationists that he had "group dynamics skills."

In our improvisational drama classes, he would do such sensitive things as interrupting an improvisation by bellowing out, "Won't somebody *help* me?" George explained to him that he was only making a gimmicky attempt to dominate the group, and he quieted down somewhat. But he continued to use such phony "sensitivity" gimmicks in dealing with his colleagues, until some of them became fairly disgusted with him.

We conducted ten weekly sessions for a group of counselors, most of whom considered themselves "group dynamics oriented." One class with this group was probably the worst fiasco we have ever had with improvisational drama.

The disintegration started with an exercise in which the people were to simply mill about on the stage saying whatever came into their heads. Instead, Stanley, a round, bouncy counselor, started discussing George. He would buttonhole another counselor and say, "How can we help George?" He quickly got several other counselors into the conversation, and they stood loudly discussing George as he continued to wander about, now saying in a distressed voice, "Why are they standing there talking about me?"

"George feels that he can't trust us!" Stanley proclaimed cheerfully. "Let's show him he can trust us."

He marshalled the group into a circle, waylaid George, and plunked him in the center. Then they performed the sensitivity cliche labeled "trust." Stanley grasped George from behind and told him to close his eyes and go limp. With his feet dragging in the center of the circle, George was passed from one person to another, all the way around and back to Stanley.

The idea of this exercise is that if no one drops the subject, his trust in the group is strengthened.

Sure enough, nobody dropped George!

Also, nobody in the group said anything about the tension in his body or the unhappy, bewildered expression evident on his face despite his closed eyes.

When George was released, he said quietly, "I don't understand why you did that. What did it mean?"

"George feels that we're not supportive to him," Stanley announced vigorously.

Supportive. No other word was needed. Efficiently and methodically, the counselors swept George from his feet and hoisted him into the air, holding his body horizontal as high as their arms would reach. They held him up there for quite a while, eliminating any doubt that they were truly a supportive group.

After this appalling exercise in canned sensitivity, the disturbed look on George's face was quite genuine, but nobody in the class mentioned it. Stanley and several other counselors felt quite smug about having made the "right" response, demonstrating their professional mastery of sensitivity. While they were in that mood, George thought, any attempt to talk them into understanding the triteness and pointlessness of what they had done would be ineffectual. So George tried to forge onward through the class. But the facile mood was set, and every subsequent activity drew stereotyped responses. George ended the class early and retired to lick his pedagogical wounds.

The group of counselors eventually learned how to use physical activity in their counseling groups. Some of them had known that what Stanley led them in doing was silly, and most of the others learned to be more discriminating and purposeful about group dynamics activities. But we doubt that Stanley ever did.

The "trust" and "support" exercises the counselors used can be effective with people who have not been spoiled by superficial exposure to them. A teacher might well use them with children. But in dealing with adults, anything that might be trite should be avoided altogether.

Twenty-One:
VARIED USES

Improvisational drama ideas have been adapted to classroom use in many ways other than full-fledged improvisational drama courses. We think that any use would be facilitated by giving a regular course of at least three months. The students would then be able to respond more freely and effectively to later uses of these techniques. But such a preparatory course is not necessary.

TEACHING CREATIVE WRITING

An outstanding creative writing teacher wanted to maintain a high level of emotional and physical involvement in her classes. She focused on playwriting. The boys she taught knew almost nothing about putting words on paper, but, after great effort on her part, many of them eventually wrote and produced dramatic scripts that were strikingly superior to any work they had done before.

The teacher had a broad repertoire of techniques for teaching playwriting, some of which were similar to those of her colleagues who were teaching improvisational drama. One technique she found effective was to have the students improvise alternatives.

One group had been talking—as inner-city boys often do—about violence and the law. They had become interested in capital punishment. One boy was given the assignment, "The court has sentenced you to death. You are on death row, and you are just about to be led to the electric chair." The boy was allowed to choose others to help him with the improvisation. After doing it once, he and the boys who had acted with him were told, "Do it a different way. Make an alternative."

In all, they did the assignment four different ways, while the tape recorder picked up the "sound track" and the teacher took a few simple notes on their physical actions. The group then discussed the four improvisations, and selected the third alternative as having been the best. As in Improvisational Drama discussions, the students formed their own esthetic values.

Using the tape and notes, several boys set out to write a script for the play. (The other boys were writing scripts from other improvised alternatives.) The improvisation provided the basis for the script, giving the boys the confidence of knowing they had a framework for their writing. But they could take off or embellish in any way they agreed on.

One boy wrote an entirely new monologue for the condemned man. It was hysterical and quite powerful—for those who could decipher it. The monologue was typewritten, single-spaced, covering almost a full sheet of paper. It had no punctuation or capitalization and very few spaces between words. More than half of the words were misspelled.

The teacher did not criticize the "mechanics" of the monologue. Rather, she suggested that the young writer choose someone to play the condemned man and give him the script to read. The writer chose a friend whom he knew was able to read; but the boy could not make out the first line. The teacher suggested that the writer try to fix his script so his friend would be able to read it. The boy panicked. But after a few days and considerable encouragement, he did rewrite the script. And then he rewrote it again after his friend still found stumbling places in it. During the rewriting, the teacher showed him such things as how to make stops and pauses with periods and commas.

It was an agonizing chore for the boy, but he did start to get a crude grasp of some of the rudiments of grammar, which he had always assumed was hopelessly over his head.

When the play was produced, he heard his friend read the passage that he had written. It was unquestionably quite good.

The applications of improvisational drama techniques to the teaching of creative writing have been many. This example should show how teachers can get ideas that work.

ALL-DAY EARLY CHILDHOOD CLASSES

We know some teachers who have used improvisational drama techniques as a way of structuring their full-day primary school classes. The day begins with warm-ups, and concludes with an ending exercise before the children go home.

During the day, appropriate exercises can be used when students seem to need energizing, relaxing, or better concentration. Improvisations can be used in many academic activities.

Teachers who have tried it tell us that this way of using the children's energies elicits unusually purposeful involvement.

AT THE ART MUSEUM

When Miss Susan Sollins became Curator of Education at the National Collection of Fine Arts in Washington, D.C., she was appalled at what a "dreary, tedious, foot-hurting experience" touring the museum was for most young children.

"Wherever I went I'd see these endless lines of school kids being herded around," she said. "It was dreadfully boring."

Miss Sollins sought the help of two teacher-administrators of the Arena Stage Children's Theater in Washington: Robert Alexander, the director, and Norman Gevanthor, the associate director. Both had taught improvisational theater techniques to teachers of art, history, literature, and science.

The two men ran a workshop for the volunteers who guide children's tours at the museum, and began a highly successful new way of conducting art tours through improvisation.

When the children first gather, the guide leads them in warm-ups, such as mirror images. Or one child might be told to "spin, spin, spin," and then, "Freeze." "Children, what would you call the statue he is making?" the guide asks the rest of the class.

After warm-ups, the tour begins. The guide urges the children to feel the works of art and, when possible, to imitate them.

Before a representational work, such as Ferdinand Pettrich's statue "The Dying Tecumseh," the children use their bodies to interpret the work.

They sometimes try to interpret physically even the most abstract works, or they might tell how an abstract work makes them feel. A picture that was essentially a square of paint with other squares faintly visible within it elicited a variety of comments:

"It makes me concentrate. It makes me think about things." "I feel cold." "I feel lonely." "I feel sad." "I feel quiet."

People connected with the program are convinced that it gives children exceptionally rich experiences in the art museum, and that they carry much of this experience home with them.[1]

Improvisation can be used to help children experience art works, animals, machines—almost anything that has a physical form. The physical involvement, concentration, and imagination necessary for these activities help the students experience what they are learning about in ways which can approach whole perception.

EMOTIONAL CONTENT

When divorced from the feelings and relationships of the people involved, the study of literature, history, and other subjects in the humanities and social sciences often produces such profound misunderstanding of content that the usefulness of what is learned is greatly reduced. Comprehension is often increased if the students can get into the feelings of the people they read about. Simple exercises such as asking children to walk like a person they have been reading about may prove valuable. Or they might act out a literary or historical event they have read about. Students can be assigned characters from films they have seen and books they have read—Ralph Moody of *Little Britches,* Christopher Robin, some of the boys in *Lord of the Flies*—and put into situations in which the group must make a decision or work together. For example, they might be asked to form a club. Or they could be told that they have been stranded together on a desert island.

Cyril Johnson, a black teacher at the Pennsylvania Advancement School used improvisational drama to launch a group of black students into a course in black identity and culture. The course seemed to be effective in helping the boys to find meaning in their common and individual experience, and to express their feelings about it.

If the teacher concentrates on making physical and emotional activity a part of his plans, ideas for improvisations will come easily and naturally.

COUNSELING

Counselors have been among the educators who have made the most extensive use of what they have learned in our workshops. Because of the way some schools are organized, counselors frequently have more flexibility in their schedules than do teachers, and are in a better position to try new things. Public school counselors who have combined improvisational drama with other group dynamics techniques report new counseling effectiveness.

THE THEATER

Needless to say, improvisation is of great value in theatrical training. We have conducted workshops for groups of amateur actors, employing the same basic structure that we use with other groups, and emphasizing physical freeing.

We have learned not to hold sessions with theater people on a stage. Their consciousness of the proscenium can lead to competitiveness and staginess, even if there is no audience. It is better to use a more intimate place that does not have such strong connotations for them.

Plays based on spontaneous improvisations provide excellent group practice. These productions usually involve doing many improvisations on a given theme or series of themes, then selecting, polishing, and combining the improvised materials into a coherent series.

SHORT WORKSHOPS

Although we believe that important change seldom, if ever, takes place in short workshops, we have conducted a good many sessions ranging in duration from three hours to two days. But as fascinating as these experiences are for us, and as excited as the participants are by the possibilities opened to them, these quickie workshops are unlikely to do much more than introduce new concepts and indicate directions for exploration.

When the people in a workshop are already working as a group on some task, we try to define the main problems of the group and give them an opportunity to explore ways of working on their problems. The workshops can never be more than a beginning. Often, participants feel that they have undergone something resembling a conversion experience. We try to encourage them to keep their feet on the ground, but some are likely to be disappointed when they find that they are still much the same as they have been.

It is essential that the leader of these workshops not let them become encounter groups. In a workshop we did with one organization, an executive had an "Aha" experience. Watching one of his employees in an improvisation, he thought, "Aha! He's paranoid! So that's why he's been causing us problems!"

During a coffee break, the executive excitedly told us of his discovery, and urged that George tell the fellow he was paranoid. We explained that the damage wrought by psychological name-calling is always hard to undo, and in a short workshop there is no chance at all. In the excitement of the experience, people sometimes get the idea that they can quickly effect "cures" that would be difficult to accomplish in years of individual therapy.

A MARATHON SPECIAL FOR GRADUATE STUDENTS

It is a familiar story in graduate schools of education. The students find their program unsatisfactory. They stay in school and make perfunctory progress toward their carrot—the combined master's degree and teaching certificate. But they are not involved. Their youthful vitality is not in it. And, like most people who feel that circumstances prevent them from being fully alive, they are bitter. They feel that the faculty—whom the more charitable students might regard as helpless pawns of the system—has let them down.

This particular class had two teachers working as a team in an experimental one-year M.A.T. program at an Ivy League graduate school of education. The program began in June with eight students, and four more joined the class in September. They were to work together for the rest of the year in a group program, helping each other to grow as teachers.

The professors started by promising all of the things sound educational theory says such a program should have: freedom, student responsibility, no arbitrary and unfair evaluations. But these good intentions fell victim to "educator's lag"—the great gap between what is known about learning and what is known about how teachers can help it to happen. In this program the weak spot was in finding concrete ways of applying educational theory.

By the end of the summer, many of the students were disenchanted with the program. Possibly in an effort to assert their authority, the professors surprised the students by giving them grades at summer's end. When the students responded with howls of outrage, the professors were unable to give them a satisfactory explanation as to why they had suddenly decided to give grades.

By October, the students were openly contemptuous, and the bewildered teachers were on the defensive. The group was only going through the motions. Probably it was not as bad as some programs at graduate schools of education, but it had fallen far short of the promises, and the grumbling students were sure they were learning nothing.

After observing several of the group's class meetings, discussing their problems with the students, and getting the nervous consent of the teachers, George agreed to try a four-hour special workshop at the request of the students.

The group was interested in two things: actually experiencing and learning about some of the new educational techniques they had thought their program would make available to them, and getting the relationships in their group straightened out as much as possible. (There were tensions between students, as well as between students and teachers.)

We started the session, with all twelve students and both teachers, with physical freeing warm-ups. They did vigorous movement to music and blind face explorations with their fingertips. Then George said, "Look about the room, please. Get up and go to somebody you do not know well, and discover his face. Do it quickly. Feel the texture of his skin. Feel it. Feel the elasticity. Discover it well. Know it. It's alive. It's important." This exercise, intended mainly to loosen physical inhibitions, turned out to be effective also in getting the group to concentrate seriously.

After doing shadow play, the class began to clap in rhythm. As they clapped, George divided them into two groups, arranging each group in a circle. Then one student was assigned to observe each group and analyze its process in the exercise called The Bomb Shelter. Each group was told that it was in a bomb shelter, that the major nations had just filled the air with missiles carrying nuclear warheads, and that the shelter had space and supplies for three more people. They were given mimeographed lists of seventeen people who were outside the shelter. The lists included a star professional athlete, an English teacher, a black militant leader, the pregnant wife of someone already in the shelter, a college student, a musician, a policeman, a cook, a mathematics teacher, a janitor, an actress, a minister, a soldier, an artist. A broad enough range of occupations was represented to stimulate conflicts in values.

"In a short time the radiation level outside your shelter will become dangerous," they were told. "You have exactly ten minutes to decide which three of these people you will admit to your shelter."

After the ten minutes were up, the groups and their observers discussed what had happened. They agreed that they had been self-centered, inconsiderate, and sloppy in their discussions. For the most part, they had not made good use of the resources within their groups.

Then George mixed the two groups and gave the same ten-minute assignment to the two new groups that were formed. In the following discussion, both groups agreed that they had improved somewhat.

Then George told them to all lie on the floor in such a way that each person's head was on another's belly. "You have two tasks: Don't laugh, and make another person laugh." Faces reddened as they rubbed the backs of their heads on bellies. A girl was the first to crack, bursting into loud, hysterical laughter. When all of them were giggling helplessly, George told them to take a ten-minute break. They had been working together for two hours.

After the intermission, George divided them into two groups again and gave them thirty minutes to discuss anything related to their graduate program. "Decide among yourselves what you're going to talk about, the problems you're going to discuss, and how you're going to arrive at your conclusions. Then carry out your plan for the discussion."

After the thirty-minute discussion, they came together in one large group, and launched the next discussion by reporting on what the smaller groups had done. One aggressive, talkative young fellow said his group had talked about "the role of personal concern and feeling for each other as individuals and how that relates to how well we function as a group."

"I finally got them to tell me to shut up," he said with apparent satisfaction.

In this final discussion, which lasted forty-five minutes, things finally started to jell. The students poured out their dissatisfactions. When the teachers tried to make excuses for their actions, the students openly said that excuses were unacceptable. Then the teachers —one of whom was chain-smoking with shaking hands—talked honestly about the problems they had encountered in trying to start a sweepingly different kind of teacher education program.

As their anger burned low, the students began to discuss their own responsibility for helping the program to succeed. They saw the incongruity of blaming teachers for the failure of a program that ostensibly emphasized student autonomy. Some of the youngsters seemed to become sympathetically aware that their teachers had suffered as well as blundered.

The group also noted that their ability to talk together had improved greatly. The step-by-step improvement had been obvious, from the first bomb shelter exercise to the second, to the small group discussions, to the final discussion by the whole group. They had become so much in tune that they no longer interrupted each other or misunderstood what others were talking about. In earlier discussions, when people agreed with what was being said, they sat deadpan, giving no indication of interest. Toward the end, their agreement was obvious from the barely perceptible nodding of heads or simply from the light in their eyes.

The workshop concluded with improvisations and activities that were expressive and enjoyable. As the glowing students left, the teacher who had been most shaken by the experience (and, as it turned out, had learned the most) stayed behind. "I saw exactly what you did with this class," he said thoughtfully, "but I don't believe it."

Although the group of students had never been close, they went to the apartment of one of them, cooked a spaghetti supper, and sat on the floor talking excitedly until 5:00 a.m.

At their next regular class meeting, the students decided to run the program themselves, using the teachers as resources. They voted to have no grades or comprehensive examinations, and they said they were willing to fight the university administration over that point if necessary. The teachers seemed very excited about the students' increased involvement.

Enthusiasm continued well into the semester, and the students held night meetings at teachers' homes, until the university administration vetoed their plan to have no grades or comprehensives. However, we are sure that the group's burst of vitality was beneficial to both students and teachers.

"WILD AND DEEP AND WONDERFUL!"

In 1968, nine alumni of the Harvard Graduate School of Education, who were attending an alumni conference in Philadelphia, came to the Advancement School for a demonstration. They didn't know what to expect, and didn't much care. They were tired; some had hangovers; they didn't know each other well; they didn't know much about our school; and none of them had ever met George before.

With no explanation, George sat them on floor cushions, started the music, and began to gyrate, as the educators watched open-mouthed and unbelieving. When George called to them to get up and dance, they were paralyzed. Insistently, George repeated the instruction. They swung into it, and for more than two hours they were absorbed in a deepening succession of experiences which left them exhausted and excited about the potential of improvisational drama.

Those we talked with afterwards said it was one of the most stimulating and enlightening experiences they had had in education. A New York City educator wrote to us of his "excitement at being in the program directed by George Mager yesterday afternoon. It was wild and deep and wonderful!"

IMPROVISING IN APPALACHIA

We could have had a special problem with the two-day workshop we held for antipoverty workers in Wilkes and Ashe counties, North Carolina. People in that area were conservative about appearance; George's floppy hair and Farnum's beard could have put up a barrier right from the first. When we checked into North Wilkesboro's hotel, before we could even get on the elevator, the desk clerk was on the telephone telling people that two hippies were in town.

For our first three-hour session, the fifteen participants were community organizers recruited from Wilkes and Ashe. We prepared the room before they arrived, putting black paper over the windows and making a crude spotlight from an ancient gooseneck lamp. Because a few of the participants were advanced in years, we used a circle of straight-backed chairs instead of floor cushions.

As the participants arrived, they were greeted at the door and asked to wait outside. When the entire group had gathered in the hall, we started the music, opened the door, welcomed them into our den, and immediately swept them into a rhythm activity. For the first half hour of the three-hour session, they were moving too fast to stop and think about how weird we looked.

For the second session of the first day, the size of the group was more than doubled by the addition of about twenty community volunteers. By this time, our original group of organizers was so enthusiastically involved that the newcomers were immediately cooperative.

On the second day, we met for the first session with the core group of fifteen organizers. For the evening session we were to meet with a large group of Ashe County volunteers. We gave the organizers a choice: they could let George lead the evening session, or they could plan and lead the session themselves. They chose to do it themselves.

These community organizers were a remarkable group of people. They were warm, noncompetitive, considerate, and intelligent. But they tended to be unassertive, and they were being called on to organize community groups to do things that had not been done in their area before. During the two days of the workshop, we concentrated on helping them to build confidence, to learn new approaches to working with people, and to deepen their perceptiveness about other people.

When they planned for the final session, they were full of imagination and enthusiasm. That evening, as the large group of volunteers started to arrive, the organizers were excited and highly nervous. But they went through with their entire plan, and the last session was very rewarding for all the participants. Afterwards, we talked with the volunteers, who were eager to discuss their wealth of interesting insights.

This Appalachian group made the most progress in a short time of any workshop group we had. On the second day, some of them told us that they had stayed awake most of the night thinking about what they learned during the first day. And some of them told us they were glad they had learned to be less suspicious of strange-looking people.

DISCOVER YOUR OWN WAYS

Every teacher can find his own ways of using improvisational drama. In this book we give only a few of the ways that we and other teachers have used. Innumerable possible variations are yet untried.

You take it from here.

NOTES

1. *New York Times,* 9 April 1969, p. 32.

Twenty-Two:
THE CREATIVE TEACHER

AN INNOVATOR'S NIGHTMARE

It is 1985. For the first time in years, silver-haired, crusty George Mager has gotten away from the school district's central administration building long enough to visit a school. The old man was once an outstanding teacher. Then attention was focused on a radical thing he was doing—a thing he called improvisational drama.

Eventually, Mager's radical thing—mellowed by the years—was immortalized in a soporific curriculum guide, and he was rewarded for his good teaching by being promoted to a job in which he did not teach.

As he dodders down the hallway of the gleaming Agnew Junior High School, Mager is pleased by the abundance of Sophisticated Educational Hardware in evidence. He particularly wants to observe a class taught by Arnold. (Teachers *must* be addressed by their first names now.) Arnold is due for promotion to an important (i.e., nonteaching) position because of his recent high score on the machine-graded test on the Improvisational Drama Curriculum Guide.

Mager opens a door and steps into a small booth from which he can observe a classroom through one-way glass. As his ancient eyes adjust to the classroom's darkness, he sees Arnold and a group of children sitting on floor cushions.

A plump girl asks, "Will we get to Believability next week, Arnold?" Arnold replies that they will if they "buckle down and finish off Concentration first."

An anguished youth cries, "Why d'we gotta have it the same every year? First we get freed up physically; then there's Concentration; then Believability . . . ."

"We do Improvisational Drama *right*!" Arnold snaps. "Any changes in the Curriculum Guide would have to come from Central Administration. As for you, you're in school, so stop thinking about things that are none of your business and *get sensitive*!

A record player blares out a jazz selection that was popular fifteen years ago. Sullen and dispirited, the children rise to their feet and surround Arnold, who begins frugging mechanically in a spotlight.

As Mager watches the grim scene, he convulses in a shudder of mortification.

PRESERVING SPONTANEITY

Obviously, this book is not the curriculum guide of that dread fantasy. We have tried to make it clear that we are not trying to tell anyone precisely how to teach. A teacher should try to approach each class in a fresh frame of mind and let it be different from any class he has ever taught before.

A series of lesson plans that gets excellent results with one group of students can be exhumed from the files and used with another group later. This is such an obvious expedient that some quite creative teachers we know have done it, with results ranging from disappointing to catastrophic.

Every teacher must create his own ways of teaching, because every teacher is different. And a teacher cannot isolate what he is from what he wants his students to learn. A child absorbs attitudes toward work, other people, and life from the adults with whom he spends the most time. If the teacher conveys the attitude, "You learn this, but I'm much too good to be interested in it," the child is unlikely to find the content meaningful. It is important for a teacher to be excited about what he is doing and to believe in it, so that children will feel caught up by the teacher's excitement and bolstered by his strength. A child can learn much by working with a person who is serious about his work and finds great pleasure in it.

HE WHO CAN, TEACHES

Most of us are to some extent the victims of bad schools. Some of those who have been most deadened by school systems are those who have spent their whole lives in them. By middle age they are principals or superintendents, afraid of change, afraid of people, afraid of life. If a person has gained much of his education in stimulating pursuits outside of schools, the chances are good that he will be able to teach creatively.

With good reason, teachers often bristle when they hear George Bernard Shaw's epigram, "He who can, does. He who cannot, teaches."[1] Actually, "he who cannot" probably should not be teaching. Teachers, like students and all other people, need to create, to be stimulated, and to learn from experience.

Shaw's epigram belittles teachers as people with no talent. A worse aspect of the educational situation is that many schools are rigged so that creative talent cannot flourish in them. Frightened, incompetent bureaucrats—the lifelong dependents of our murderous educational systems who "make policy" in so many schools—have unscrupulous ways of harrassing teachers. Even among those who find it politically feasible to call themselves liberals, the attitude often is, "We're all for innovation, as long as you don't do anything different."

The teaching profession is hurt by the attitude of benign contempt with which teachers are regarded by many citizens (including themselves). And the stereotypical defense raised by educators against that contempt has only hurt the profession more. They have raised barriers against those who would teach by pretentiously affecting the trappings of "professionalism." Many of the deadly education courses a person must suffer through to get his bureaucratic teaching ticket are an affront to anyone with the ability, character, and energy to become a fine teacher.

Equally false is the dilettante notion that teaching is easy for one whose beliefs are sufficiently liberal or whose heart is in the right place. This book affirms that teaching is a demanding and complex art.

At the least, an adequate teacher should like and understand his students, be concerned with his own continued growth in self-understanding, and be able to create in media relevant to what he is teaching.

GETTING IMPROVISATIONAL DRAMA INTO THE SCHOOLS

Despite the obstacles raised by the envious and incompetent foes of change, people in different places and different kinds of schools are teaching improvisational drama. Alternative schools are rising, and we hope that public education funds will soon be pushed in their direction, either through a voucher-type system or through the allotting of portions of public school district funds to alternative schools. Established schools often react to competition from alternatives by allowing more freedom to teachers and students. Already improvisational drama appears widely (though not deeply) known enough that many schools will permit it to be taught, although often the teacher must have a thick skin in dealing with administrators.

A teacher in a Philadelphia Junior High School started teaching our course simply by starting to teach it. Learning of it immediately, the pompous principal was aghast. The teacher laughed off his principal and continued the course.

Whatever governments or systems do, changing schools for the better requires teachers with courage. We hope there will be many of them.

People have only isolated moments of education in a school. Improvisational drama is one way of helping to increase the frequency of these moments of discovery. All effective ways of doing this have something in common: They enable the teacher to go with, not against, the flow of students' creative energy.

NOTES

1. George Bernard Shaw, "Maxims for Revolutionists," in *Man and Superman* (1903; Baltimore: Penguin Books, 1952), p. 260.

SELECTIVE BIBLIOGRAPHY

Allport, Gordon W. *Personality: A Psychological Interpretation.* New York: Henry Holt and Co., 1937. Includes an enlightening study of expressive behavior.

Barnfield, Gabriel. *Creative Drama in Schools.* London: Macmillan, 1968. Good suggestions about how to work with younger children. Many interesting activities suggested.

Boleslavsky, R. *Acting: The First Six Lessons.* New York: Theater Arts Books, 1963. Particularly valuable for teachers who lack formal training in drama. Explanation of basic principles.

Bruce, V. *Dance and Drama in Education.* London: Pergamon Press, 1965. Valuable for teachers working with younger students. Fine exercises.

Courtney, Richard. *Play, Drama and Thought.* London: Cassell and Co., 1970. Primarily theoretical and historical.

Held, Jack Preston. *Improvisational Acting.* Belmont, California: Wadsworth Publishing Co., 1971. Some good suggestions for improvisations and exercises.

Herron, R. E., and Sutton-Smith, Brian (with chapters by other authors). *Child's Play.* New York: John Wiley & Sons, 1971. Collected readings on a broad spectrum of theories of play.

Hodgson, John, and Richards, Ernest. *Improvisation.* London: Methuen and Co., 1967. Both theoretical material and suggested activities. Also presents studies of work done with students in British public schools.

Maslow, Abraham H. *Toward a Psychology of Being.* New York: Van Nostrand Reinhold Co., 1968.

Missildine, W. Hugh. *Your Inner Child of the Past.* New York: Simon and Schuster, 1963.

Moore, Sonia. *The Stanislavski System.* New York: Viking Press, 1969.

Moreno, J. L. *Psychodrama.* New York: Beacon House, 1946. Describes what improvisational drama is not.

Simon, Sidney B.; Howe, Leland; and Kirschenbaum, Howard. *Values Clarification: A Handbook of Practical Strategies for Teachers and Students.* New York: Hart Publishing Co., 1972. A collection of exercises, many of which are valuable for use within the improvisational drama structure.

Smilansky, Sara. *The Effects of Sociodramatic Play on Disadvantaged Children.* New York: John Wiley & Sons, 1968.

Spolin, Viola. *Improvisation for the Theater.* Evanston, Ill.: Northwestern University Press, 1963. A virtually inexhaustible bank of ideas for exercises, as well as important theory on theater games.

Way, Brian. *Development Through Drama.* London: Longmans, Green and Co., 1967; New York: Humanities Press, 1967. Expounds important new theories of development. Sees improvisational drama as a course that must be nonlinear in its development.